ABUSE OF POWER

A memoir by

Frank Shortt

© 2012 Frank Shortt

Front cover painting by Mira Reichl

All rights reserved. No part of this publication may be reproduced in any form or by any means—graphic, electronic or mechanical, including photocopying, recording, taping or information storage and retrieval systems—without the prior written permission of the author.

ISBN: 978-0-9572585-0-1

Published by Shortt Forefathers Publishing 2012

Dedicated first and fore mostly to my ever loving Wife

Sally

And My Children

Jalisco, Natasha, Zabrina, Kristian and Azariah

And

My son Kelly

Contents

Prologue	*vii*
Chapter One THE HISTORY OF THE POINT INN	1
Chapter Two THE GATHERING STORM	14
Chapter Three THE MISSING FAX	18
Chapter Four THE STING	27
Chapter Five FIRST ASSAULT ON THE POINT INN, 3RD AUGUST 1992	33
Chapter Six SECOND ASSAULT ON THE POINT INN, 12TH FEBRUARY 1993	38
Chapter Seven THIRD ASSAULT ON THE POINT INN, SEPTEMBER 30, 1994	41
Chapter Eight DEATH THREATS AND ARSON	51
Chapter Nine MY TRIAL	56
Chapter Ten MOUNTJOY PRISON COMPLEX	79

Chapter Eleven
MY APPEAL 85

Chapter Twelve
PRISON TRIALS AND TRIBULATIONS 93

Chapter Thirteen
FELLOWSHIP OF THE JOY 100

Chapter Fourteen
THE PRISON GUARDS 105

Chapter Fifteen
DIGGING THE TRENCHES 118

Chapter Sixteen
MY VINDICATION 131

Chapter Seventeen
THE CHILDREN 139

Chapter Eighteen
HORIZONS REACHED 148

EPILOGUE 155

Appendix One
Letter to Minister of Justice Mr. Padraig Flynn 158

Appendix Two
Evidence Of Superintendent Brian N. Kenny 161

Appendix Three
Frank Shortt's Evidence 180

Appendix Four
Letters to Nora Owen 194

Prologue

In a rural village in County Donegal, Ireland, a two-hundred strong force of Gardai lay in wait in the shadows around the Point Inn nightclub. They were armed with sledgehammers, batons and guns, and dressed in riot armour. The unsuspecting proprietor, Frank Shortt, along with his young clientele, were about to face the biggest Garda assault operation the country had ever seen. Helmets on, visors down, the stalking predators awaited the call...

***

"Francis Shortt, you have been convicted on all counts open to the jury by them and I will impose a sentence of three years imprisonment on each count to run concurrently, and a further fine of £10,000." – **Gerard Buchanan, Judge. Circuit Criminal Court, Dublin. 1st March 1995.**

These were the chilling words which shook me to the core and sealed my fate and that of my family. The words that sent the reporters rushing to catch the deadline for their newspapers. The words which sent the triumphant forty-three man Donegal contingent of the Garda Siochana winging their way home in delight – their long, dogged campaign ultimately rewarded, their prey securely in prison. These were the words which stole the freedom I had enjoyed for sixty years and thrust me into a shameful prison cell.

The Garda Siochana offensive against me and my legitimate nightclub, the Point Inn, Quigley's Point, County Donegal, spanned three years. During that time countless Garda man-hours were expended to build a case against me. These operations, plus the many court hearings, must have cost the Irish taxpayer millions of punts.

The Garda Siochana, the very people whom we are expected to look up to with respect as a law abiding police force, appeared to act with impunity as far as I and my legitimate business were concerned. No other nightclub owner, throughout the entire country, was treated in a similar fashion. Despite soft drugs – and hard drugs, which never were discovered at the Point Inn – being found in many other nightclubs, no other nightclub owner was ever jailed.

Prior to the Garda actions against my business, the local newspapers in Donegal were carrying reports of a major transfer of Garda personnel out of the county for relocation in the areas of Dublin, Cork and Limerick where crime was reaching alarming proportions. It seemed that the Minister for Justice was of the opinion that the surplus of Garda personnel in Donegal could be better deployed where crime was rife. However, most of the Gardaí had set up homes in Donegal at that stage and were reluctant to leave. Around that time, the Gardai suddenly became very active: setting up road blocks, checking licenses, motor insurance and tax, and following up with summonses. And of course, the actions against my business commenced and didn't let up for three years, until I was imprisoned and my nightclub maliciously burned down. Was there a correlation between the Garda actions against my business and their unwillingness to be transferred out of their cushy postings in quiet Donegal?

At the same time, there was increasing pressure brought to bear on the Garda Siochana by politicians to successfully prosecute a high profile case in order to demonstrate to the public that they were not going soft on the drugs epidemic which was sweeping our country. One can recall similar pressure on the British police to nail someone for the Guildford bomb.

It seems as if a few Gardaí, cold and cynical, set about the task of making me into a criminal, fabricating charges and concocting evidence. It developed into a determined and corrupt use and abuse of power against an ordinary citizen where the due processes of law and order were violated. There must be few other cases in this State where three years of unmerited police actions had been indulged in with such vindictiveness and with such extravagance and expense. Systematically, the Gardaí, aided and abetted by other State bodies and institutions, ruined my business and practically bankrupted me. It must now be obvious that I was a convenient victim for Garda and political manoeuvring and window dressing.

A suitable sacrificial lamb.

In later days, after I had won my freedom and been cleared of all wrong-doing, I paid close attention to the Morris Tribunal. It shocked me to read the testimony of witnesses like Sheenagh McMahon, the estranged wife of one of the main detectives involved in my case. Apparently both Detective McMahon and Superintendent Lennon (who was still only an inspector when he gave his damning evidence against me) were involved with the making, distributing and planting of bombs across County Donegal with the aim of discovering the devices themselves and winning promotion.

Mrs McMahon also stated that her husband Noel had kicked her and punched her and even went as far as putting a gun to her head and threatening to blow her brains out. He pulled back the hammer and clicked it; the gun wasn't loaded. He is believed to have said the same thing to another man, stating that he would "blow his brains out".

It was a widespread belief amongst the public in Donegal that certain Gardaí were "untouchable and dangerous to cross". And it was also believed that there was no point making complaints to Garda management or the Garda Complaints Board as there was a culture in the force of "Blue Silence". I can't help but wonder if public opinion has changed at all, or if the Gardaí themselves are still behaving in such a manner as to warrant such suspicion.

When my wife first read the draft of this book she remarked that it contained much anger. I responded that injustice breeds anger. I thought much about suppressing this anger but then that would have stifled my true feelings regarding this entire affair. Readers would want to know my real displeasure and exasperation rather than a colourful display of suppressed feelings. In the light of the disgraceful and contemptible treatment which I and my family have been forced to endure over the past several years, I see no reason why I should not give vent to my feelings simply to avoid annoying the Garda Siochana, the DPP, the judiciary, my jailers and some politicians.

By the time the reader has come to the end of my book there will be no doubt that I suffered state brutality and gross injustice.

Chapter One
The history of the Point Inn

My name is Frank Bosco Shortt and I am an honest businessman. Yet over the course of three years, a handful of Gardaí, cold and cynical, set about the task of framing me as a criminal. There must be few other cases in this State where three years of unmerited police actions had been indulged in with such vindictiveness, extravagance and expense. Systematically the Gardaí, aided and abetted by other state bodies and institutions, ruined my business and all but bankrupted me. And capped it off by sending me to prison for three years.

Now I have been cleared of all charges, I wish to tell my story.

Quigley's Point is a small hamlet of scattered houses on the Inishowen Peninsula in County Donegal. It nestles at the foot of the mountains on the northern shore of beautiful Lough Foyle. Buncrana, Carndonagh and Moville are the closest towns on the Free State side of the border. Derry, nine miles away on the other side of the border, is the closest city.

Our little village might very well have enjoyed anonymity were it not for my nightclub, the Point Inn, which placed Quigley's Point "on the map" – first as a popular venue for young people and later as the scene of three infamous Garda raids and the ongoing police harassment of myself and my customers.

My parents were called Bernard and Cecelia and they had many children together. Growing up I had 5 brothers (Jim, Raphael, Paddy, Louis and Brian) and 2 sisters (Teresa and Cecelia).

Many of the Shortt family standing outside The Point Inn in 1964' From left to right, Frank Shortt, 3rd from left, Bernard Shortt, 6th from left, Sister Vianney (my Aunt), 7th from left, my mother Cecelia, 8th from left, my brother Jim, 9th from left Ned (my uncle), 10th from left, Brian.

The Point Inn had a long history as a place of hospitality and entertainment. The Shortts, my great grandfather James and his wife Bella, acquired the original licensed premises sometime near the start of the last century. In the nineteenth century, the old inn was a halting station, a halfway house, for stage coaches, herders of livestock and other highway traffic plying their business between Carndonagh, Moville and Derry. Many was the propertied gentleman, crofter, herder and fisherman who must have rubbed shoulders in our snuggery over a pint of ale in days of yore.

As a young lad in 1944, I well remember my uncle Pat buying rabbits in large quantities from local hunters for export to our food-rationed neighbours across the water. Even if there was hardship, those were the good old days. There was not too much money around, so there was not too much worry either.

My father Bernard Shortt sitting with his two dogs outside the Point Inn in 1982, he was 90 years old in this picture.

However, that traditional pattern of life was passing away. The one certainty we all face, apart from death, is change. Present day town and village life scarcely resembles that of fifty years ago. Even in the past twenty years, our society and customs have changed dramatically. I'm sure the other grandfathers and grandmothers alive today, like ourselves, sadly lament the passing of those "good auld days".

The Point Inn in the winter of 1969 I believe.

When the lounge bar and women's liberation arrived in Ireland, old pubs were converted into roadhouses and new-fangled saloons. And so the Point Inn moved with the times – evolving from its nineteenth century vintage (a long heritage of which few Irish nightclubs can boast). We were proud to be the pioneers who introduced traditional music and singing into the roadhouse environment in Donegal. Many of our venerable customers will recall the wonderful and exciting music of The Cottage Folk, a local Derry group who entertained many people from near and far in our traditional Cottage Bar during the late sixties and early seventies. The names of Speedy and Joe Fox need no introduction to many of the old timers in Donegal and Derry; their outstanding musical talents and *blarney* brought a whole new sense of enjoyment into the lives of many people.

This is what the inside of the Point Inn looked like in the Seventies, sometime before the bombing.

Whilst working as manager for my father in the Point Inn I met a charming young lady by the name of Sally Kelly. She attended big nights in the Point Inn in the sixties, travelling there from Carndonagh with friends. Shortly after we began to date and on the 30th November 1967 we married in her local Chapel in Carndonagh.

The day I married my wife Sally on 30th November 1967. To our left is my brother Rafael who married us.

Then came the troubles in Northern Ireland, to cast a dark shadow over people's lives. That shadow also fell on the southern side of the border. Our no-warning bomb arrived on the night of 16th December 1973, in the guise of a large milk churn packed with explosives.

My father detected the awesome weapon of destruction in time to evacuate both the Inn and the whole village around. I was sitting in my own home six miles away, and the detonation rattled my windows and doors. I drove immediately to the Inn and was outraged at what confronted me. The darkness, only slightly lit by a nearby street lamp, was still heavy with dust and smoke. The front wall of the building was blown inwards and the roof of the building was gone. A frightening sight was the contents of my mother's wardrobe and bed dangling from the upper branches of a high tree in front of the building. Thanks to my father's quick actions, nobody had been hurt.

The centuries-old Inn was completely destroyed, and could not be restored. Our family was almost as shattered. This was our first bitter taste of the conflict which was to rage on in the North for many more years. However, it was not to be our last. We grew to learn the harsh reality of living next door to a divided and strife-torn people.

*The Point Inn lying in ruins
after the IRA bomb blast of 1973.*

The Irish government and Garda Siochana were very helpful to us in our moment of need. The ruined building was demolished to make way for a new beginning. We saved some of the old stones and red bricks for inclusion in decorative work on the new building, for old time's sake. Compensation was agreed with the government and within the space of eighteen months a state-of-the-art nightclub had replaced the ruin. We were once again under way and we were once again the innovators – this time, we introduced top class cabaret to the north-west.

Pictured after the 1973 bombing with Sally (to my left) Paddy, (4th from left) my Father (5th from left), and Louis (6th from left).

The Point Inn in the time of the Cabarets in the Mid-late Seventies and Eighties.

I do believe the many years of cabaret and dancing which followed helped our customers overcome the sense of frustration and hopelessness that flowed from the troubles in the North. Many will never forget the sparkling performances given by The Dubliners, Tony Kenny, Dickie Rock, The Furey Brothers, Joe Cuddy, Colm 'C.T.' Wilkinson, Geraldine Brannigan... to name but a few. And, of course, from the local scene we had such wonderful entertainers as Mike McWilliams, Willie Laughlin, Esther McClintoch, and the internationally recognised McLaughlin School of Dancing. The honours list would not be complete without a special mention of our resident band The Trade Winds, and last but not least our wonderful presenter and MC, Don Doherty from the Plantation City itself!

The Dubliners attending the wedding of our friends Tommy and Carmel Weddick. For many years the Shortt family were good friends of the Dubliners and on a few occasions they played in the Point Inn. They would also occasionally stay in my house in Redcastle, Co. Donegal.

However, all good things eventually come to an end. People's tastes in music and entertainment never stay the same.

We at the Point Inn endeavoured to stay abreast of the changing times. In the past we had mostly got it right but as the years passed and the competition intensified we sometimes also got it wrong. Mistakes were costly, especially in capital cost of equipment, furnishings and decor. Added to that, the nightclub scene in Northern Ireland was opening up, mainly due to the relaxing of the licensing laws across the border.

The Point Inn around the year 1985

It was around this time that the International Fund for Ireland appeared on the scene. For many hard-pressed businesses, this organisation was most welcome. It was the brain-child of certain concerned Irish politicians, along with their counterparts in the United States, Canada, Australia and – later on – the EU. These politicians felt an effort ought to be made to assist those businesses in the twelve northern counties which had suffered from the Northern Ireland troubles. This assistance would be backed with hard cash in the form of grants. In the case of grant aid for tourism projects, businesses located in the six counties south of the border would be allowed to seek IFI funding through Bord Failte, the Irish Tourist Board.

In 1990, the Point Inn approached the IFI for help. The fund agreed to examine the proposed development of a camp park on our lands running down to the seashore of Lough Foyle, adjacent to The Point Inn. We hired a firm of architects who prepared plans for the development of a state-of-the-art camping complex, costing £500,000. The complex would comprise sixty parking sites accessed by paved service roads. Each site would have underground hook-ups to water, sewage, electricity, telephone and satellite TV. A large service block would contain reception, toilets, showers, jacuzzi, sauna, gaming room, TV room and the watchman's apartment. There would be two tennis courts, crazy golf course, children's play area and barbeque stands. The plans were approved by Donegal County Council and to our delight Bord Failte sanctioned IFI cash grant aid of £221,000. We were delighted with the favourable turn of events and quickly arranged the necessary additional funding from a commercial bank in order to get the program up and running. The construction of the camp complex began in 1991.

Sally and I with two old friends John and Mary Gillespie at the Listowel Races in 1966.

I had left the nightclub business several years earlier in order to set up a new venture in shellfish culture, but after the sudden tragic death of my brother, Louis, in March 1991, I once again took over the management of The Point Inn, in Quigley's Point. The business was not doing all that well so I decided to undertake a major renovation. The IFI aid did not cover that, so it was necessary to mortgage our family home, to the tune of £50,000. The nightclub was closed down during the entire winter of 1991/92 in order to facilitate the development work.

My brother Louis and I cruising Lough Erne in his boat, 1984.

Thematic decor was the "in thing" in pub development in the big cities at the time, so as part of our image, we opted for a dungeon theme! By the time we had completed the transformation, customers could be forgiven for thinking that they were in the Bastille. A full-size guillotine had been constructed in the middle of the floor, surrounded by a drink stand. (After a certain time at night, some of our customers would claim to see the ghostly shadow of Maximilien Robespierre lead Queen Marie-Antoinette up the scaffold to meet her doom.) Along one wall, we fabricated old-style prison cells with iron bars, inside each of which we placed dummy convicts. There was also a set of stocks – another great attraction. I used to joke about our stocks saying that they could come in handy in the event that we might have to subdue an overactive or frisky customer.

Altogether, the atmosphere was a mix of old medieval custom and modern nightclub mania – quite a bizarre mixture but nevertheless very memorable and powerful. The bar counter was constructed from the old red bricks which had been salvaged from the bombed-out building in 1974. The bar countertop and the overhead canopy had been ingeniously carpentered by our craftsmen out of Old Russian Yellow Pine timber salvaged from the ruins of the old seaport in Lisahally outside Derry. At each end of the nightclub we had constructed two large open hearth fireplaces and here again we used old materials from the bombings. When our discos were operating these two large turf and log fires were a great attraction to our customers.

After a few minor improvements were made at his suggestion, the Chief Fire officer, Frank Kerrane, declared that we fully complied with all fire regulations.

We re-opened our new theme nightclub on Easter Saturday, 18th April 1992, following a costly advertising promotion. Our newspaper advertisements specifically stated, among other things, that we were reserving admission to those over twenty three years of age.

The plan, of course, was to discourage under-eighteens. In reality, we did not refuse admission to anyone who appeared to be over eighteen years of age.

An army helicopter landing on our back lawn in 1992 to investigate the discovery of a World War II bomb discovered along the shore of Lough Foyle a few hundred metres from our house. This landing took place shortly after the re-opening of the Point Inn in 1992.

On our opening night, we were well supported by the young disco-going community from both sides of the border. I felt confident that we had once again reversed the downward trend of our business and were well on the road to recovery.

Chapter Two
THE GATHERING STORM

My optimism on that opening night was to be short lived. At 12.45 am, the local sergeant of the Garda Siochana, John McPhillips, brushed past me at the main entrance in what I had come to know as his usual arrogant and dismissive fashion. Sergeant McPhillips h a d recently taken over at Muff Garda Station which controlled the sub-district in which our nightclub was situated. During the previous year, prior to our closure for the winter, this Garda had subjected our business – and, I might add, all of the licensed premises in his new "patch" – to unusual surveillance and inspections.

This night, he asked me if the Inn had an exemption order, to which I responded that such exemptions were not granted for Saturday nights. He proceeded to inspect our premises, finding both our bars to be already closed, in accordance with the law.

On his way out he approached me again at the cash desk and stated loudly enough for everyone around to hear: "Get your house in order." I could see our young customers were startled by the tone of his voice, so I asked to speak to him privately outside. I requested that he clarify his comment. In answer, he gave me a loud dressing down in a very arrogant and overbearing manner. I inquired as to what aspect of my legitimate nightclub was not in compliance with the law. Once again he snapped: "Get your house in order."

There and then, I decided that if this type of unwarranted Garda surveillance was to continue then our new nightclub business was bound to fail. I telephoned the superintendent in charge of our district, Brian Kenny, on Monday 20th April 1992, and requested an appointment. He agreed without hesitation.

My wife and I travelled to Buncrana on the 21st April and met with Superintendent Kenny in his office. The superintendent had only recently taken up his post in Buncrana so we briefed him on our background and on our business. We went on to express our concerns about Sergeant John McPhillips and how his attitude and behaviour might affect our business. Superintendent Kenny was most courteous and agreed to help us in whatever way he could. He expressed his private opinion that Sergeant McPhillips did have a "thing" about public houses, but seemed surprised that the sergeant had not even given us a honeymoon period for the opening of our new disco.

Not only was my complaint a futile exercise but it appeared to infuriate Sergeant McPhillips, who intensified his inspections. During the course of the weeks that followed, our nightclub was inspected every night without exception by either the sergeant or his subordinates. By mid-May, it was clear that young people were taking exception to these constant intrusions and had deserted our nightclub for ones where they were free to enjoy themselves without ongoing Garda surveillance. On Sunday 10th May 1992, there was a grand total of nineteen customers at our disco. We were in crisis.

(Incidentally, an inspector from the fire department arrived unexpectedly in May 1992 shortly after Sergeant McPhillips began to pressurise our business. Usually, inspectors only visited licensed premises during August or September, in preparation for the annual licensing courts in September. The inspector insisted on extensive alterations, such as the demolition of our kitchen as it could impede the free flow of people in an emergency and installation of fire doors where ordinary sturdy doors had sufficed for years. Large areas of wall mirrors had to be removed as they might cause confusion in an emergency. Most incredible of all, he insisted that our bulk gas and central heating fuel tanks be removed from the rear of the building. Those tanks were regularly checked by competent technicians; both were surrounded by six feet high brick walls and had been passed as safe by that same inspector for many years. At the time both tanks were practically full of gas and central heating oil and so had to be pumped out. We were instructed to complete all aspects of this work and more without delay or an objection would be lodged immediately against our Public Dancing License and Restaurant Certificate. I immediately employed a firm, at substantial cost, to complete all of the fire department's demands.)

During the course of the following week I discussed our difficulties with my associates in the nightclub business, particularly those in Dublin.

It seemed that the entertainment industry and the world of fashion were redefining the world for young people, and anyone who ignored the trends would simply go to the wall. Several years earlier we had introduced cabaret from the big cities into the north-west. A few years later we had introduced the revolutionary "Big Apple Disco" which I had borrowed from my experience of New York nightlife. (Neither of these innovations incurred the wrath of An Garda Siochana.)

Now, once again the time was ripe for a further new innovation. This time it was to be the new music sensation which was sweeping across Europe and England. Rave.

There is nothing mysterious about rave music – at least not to our young people, who have been brought up in a world which practically runs on electronics. It uses synthesizers, a keyboard instrument in which speech, music or other sounds are produced electronically. The beat is picked up by flashing psychedelic lights.

Since the Point Inn started the rave discos back in 1992, similar discos have become an integral part of nightclub life throughout the whole of Ireland. (Although, as the term "rave" seems to inspire panic in certain people – especially the Gardaí – these discos have renamed themselves "Fantasia" or "Dance Night" or "House Music", etc.) The rave discos which we held in the Point Inn were mild affairs indeed, compared with the hyped-up rave extravaganzas presently being run week-in, week-out in most of the large nightclub complexes throughout this country. Rave is the soundtrack to endless television advertisements. Every record sales outlet boasts substantial revenues from the sales of such music. Why then, did the rave discos in our nightclub attract such incredible harassment from the Garda Siochana?

The Point Inn began its rave discos on Saturday night, 16th May 1992. Our young clientele once again supported us and flooded back in significant numbers to our nightclub.

As also did the Gardaí.

The Point Inn around the time the nightclub opened. Early Nineties.

Chapter Three
THE MISSING FAX

You know my methods, Watson.
The Memoirs of Sherlock Holmes

On Saturday, 16th May 1992, the Point Inn fought back by opening the first rave disco.

At 1.15am, Sgt. John McPhillips made his usual nightly inspection, yet again finding our bars closed in compliance with the law.

On the 17th May 1992, just one month after our first meeting with Sergeant Kenny, I was obliged to write to him again, drawing his attention to the ongoing hounding of our business by Sgt. McPhillips. In my letter I told the Superintendent that I did not expect to get a fair deal from this man but that, for the present, I was prepared to leave the problem in his, the superintendent's, hands.

I offered to attend at the superintendent's office with my solicitor in an effort to determine what we were doing wrong in our nightclub. I suggested that Sergeant McPhillips was free to attend if he so wished. But there was no relaxation in the sergeant's aggressive attitude towards me and my business. The harassment was practically continuous.

Then, three Sundays later, on the night of the 7th June 1992, Sgt. McPhillips, along with seven other Gardaí, set up a check point at 10.30pm on the road from Derry, close to The Point Inn. He was apparently targeting the young people travelling to my nightclub. (At my trial, he told the court: "We asked people who we stopped, some of the people, if they were going to the Point Inn.") As Sergeant McPhillips later said in court, no illegal substances were seized and no arrests were made. The check point remained in position until it was time to inspect the nightclub itself.

Accompanied by the same seven uniformed Gardaí, Sergeant McPhillips entered the Point Inn at 1am and commenced an illegal search of our nightclub. I asked him if he had a search warrant but he completely ignored me, as if such trivial matters were beneath him. His attitude displayed the arrogance which I had grown to expect from this sergeant. There was nothing surreptitious about it, nothing cloak and dagger – not even a passing gesture of apology or concern for the embarrassment which he and his men were causing. This man made a virtue of his arrogance.

The team of Gardai spent an hour disrupting the dancing, searching young people, shining bright torches into their faces. Sometime afterwards Sergeant McPhillips asked to see me in private. He informed me that the search had not revealed any illegal drugs, and he wanted to return and search the club again when the function ended. I consented.

Upon their return at 2.15am they searched under the seat cushions and emptied all of the ashtrays. At the time I did not know the purpose of this, but apparently they were looking for roaches, the silver tips used to smoke reefers, a cannabis-loaded cigarette. When that search was over, I asked the sergeant if he or any of his team had found any illegal drugs or traces of usage which might indicate that illegal drugs were being used in our nightclub. He said that he had found nothing.*

> *Did Sergeant John McPhillips and the other seven Gardaí violate my constitutional rights or break the law by searching my premises on the night of the 7th June 1992? They certainly did. Let us look at those sections of our Constitution and laws which protect my civil rights, and of course yours also.

Article 40 (3) of our Constitution states:
> *The State guarantees in its laws to respect, and, as far as practicable, by its laws to defend and vindicate the personal rights of the citizen. The State shall, in particular, by its laws protect as best it may from unjust attack and, in the case*

of injustice done, vindicate the life, person, good name, and property rights of every citizen.

Misuse of Drugs Act, 1977
Section 23 states:

A member of the Garda Siochana who with reasonable cause suspects that a person is in possession in contravention of this Act of a controlled drug, may without warrant ----
(a) Search the person and, if he considers it necessary for that purpose, detain the person for such time as is reasonably necessary.
(b) Search any vehicle, vessel or aircraft in which he suspects that such drug may be found and for the purpose of carrying out the search may, if he thinks fit, require the person who for the time being is in control of such vehicle, vessel or aircraft to bring it to a stop and when stopped to refrain from moving it, or in case such vehicle, vessel or aircraft is already stationery, to refrain from moving it.

Section 26 states:

If a Justice of the District Court or a Peace Commissioner is satisfied by information on oath of a member of the Garda Siochana that there is reasonable ground for suspecting that ---
(a) a person is in possession in contravention of this Act on any premises of a controlled drug, a forged prescription or a duly issued prescription which has been wrongfully altered and that such drug or prescription is on a particular premises, such Justice or commissioner may issue a search warrant mentioned in subsection (2) of this section.

The following day, 8th June 1992, the letter below was faxed by me to the Garda Station, Buncrana, at 12.11pm. Fax machines produce a paper printout verifying that the document has been transmitted. The printout in respect of my fax is stapled to the original letter and both are on file with my solicitors. For the benefit of the reader I outline as follows a duplicate of the details which appear on my printout.

TRANSACTION REPORT				P. 01	
8 - JUN - 92 MON 12.11					
DATE	START	RECEIVER	TX TIME	PAGES	NOTE
8 - JUN	12.10	353 7761555	52"	1	OK

The accompanying letter reads as follows:

08 - JUN - 92   MON 12:10   P.01

THE POINT INN

Quigley's Point, Co. Donegal

ENTERTAINMENT CENTRE OF THE NORTH-WEST

Contact: F. B. Shortt   077-82400

FAX Transmission to: 077-61686

Superintendent Brian N. Kenny

Garda Siochana

Buncrana

08 June 1992

> *Dear Superintendent Kenny,*
> *At 1.05 a.m. this morning three Garda patrol cars converged on our premises and a raid on our premises was carried out by eight Gardaí under the supervision of Sgt. John McPhillips.*

Our premises were thoroughly searched twice, once while our paying customers were present and later at 2.15 a.m. when our customers had departed. The reason given was "we have reason to believe that drugs are being consumed on your premises."
I consider this action by Sgt. McPhillips, in a long series of actions, to smack of "vendetta" and harassment. It is a direct insult to my quality of management and indeed to the position which I hold as a member of the Moville /Greencastle Environmental Group. My record over the past few years has been well documented on TV , radio and press in my efforts to protect our environment from pollution and it would be totally out of character for me to condone or acquiesce in the pollution of our young people with drugs. My wife, who helps me in management, is chairperson of the local Country Women's Association as well as being a practicing nurse, is deeply offended by the inferences and insinuations involved in the raid. We consider this raid, plus all its ramifications, to be an extreme and deep insult to the Shortt name in Quigley's Point.
Was this morning's raid inspired solely by Sergeant McPhillips or was it ordered from a higher level? It is imperative that I meet you as soon as possible in order to resolve this ongoing problem. I now invite you personally to inspect my premises.

Yours sincerely,

Frank B. Shortt, FCA
Managing Director

This faxed letter was received at Buncrana Garda Station on 8th June 1992 at precisely 12.10 p.m. The date and time appearing at the top of this document (08 - JUN - 92 MON 12.10 P. 01) was recorded not by my own machine, but by the receiving fax machine in the Garda station.

I always follow up faxes with a telephone call in order to ensure that the message has been received. So I telephoned to Supt. Kenny and he duly confirmed receipt of the fax. He agreed to come to the Point Inn for a meeting the following day.

On that Tuesday, Superintendent Kenny arrived. My wife and I held a lengthy discussion with him in our office. First, I drew the superintendent's attention to the original of the letter which I had faxed to him the previous day. Once again he confirmed receipt of that fax. I specifically drew his attention to the final paragraph. He was emphatic that he had not issued instructions that our nightclub be searched for illegal drugs by Sgt. McPhillips and a team of Gardaí. He confirmed that the sergeant had taken it upon himself to carry out the search. I noted the superintendent's remarks on the bottom of my letter.

I then told him we had prepared an agenda as follows:

1. In my opinion the Garda adopted a ham-fisted approach last Sunday night.
2. My civil rights were violated and no Search Warrant was even deemed necessary. In fact, the entire approach of Sgt. McPhillips towards our business is offensive and is a clear violation of my Constitutional Rights.
3. The fact that the drug culture has now set up their den in The Point Inn has not been proved. According to my information the pushers and users shed all their drugs immediately the police enter a premises. Yet the search last Sunday night by the Gardaí revealed no traces whatsoever of illegal drugs having been in our nightclub.
4. All discos are potential centres for drug pushers. My son and daughter, who occasionally go to other discos, tell me that they and their friends were approached many times to purchase drugs. On one recent occasion they were offered heroin in a Letterkenny nightclub.
5. At the Drug Seminar in Moville last night one woman wondered why the police were not coming down with a ton of

bricks on the importers and pushers (drug Mafia). Surely the proper police approach ought to be to cut off the drug threat at source.

6. Alcohol - This is equally as big a threat, if not in fact more devastating, than the drug threat to our society. Why is it that 13, 14 & 15 year olds continue to get away with drunken behaviour in our nightclubs? When The Point Inn reopened at Easter our press ads specifically made reference to the fact that nobody under 23 years of age would gain entry. Yet Sgt. McPhillips felt it necessary to read the riot act to me that same night.

7. Double standards adopted towards different nightclubs.

I requested that our discussion be centred around this agenda. The superintendent agreed. The first two items related mainly to the unacceptable behaviour of Sgt. McPhillips toward me and my business. As you will recall, my wife and I had already met with the superintendent only seven weeks earlier in connection with the unacceptable behaviour of this sergeant, and had written again to the superintendent only three weeks before. Once again Supt. Kenny promised to help by talking to Sgt. McPhillips.

We then discussed the problem of illegal drugs which were sweeping Ireland. The sergeant told us that illegal drugs were mainly found in pubs and nightclubs. I said we were aware of this threat and that we were concerned not only for our business, but for the wellbeing of our children. My wife told the sergeant about a seminar on illegal drugs which both of us had attended in Moville the previous evening. That seminar had been given by three Gardaí from Supt. Kenny's district, two of whom were known to us – Sergeant P.J. Hallinan and Sergeant Jim Moore of Community Relations. We assured Superintendent Kenny that we were deeply opposed to illegal drugs.

I suggested that we place large posters all around our nightclub warning customers about the dangers of illegal drugs. Some posters would outline the health risks associated with taking drugs. Other posters would warn that any customers found taking or dealing in drugs on our property would be handed over without delay to the Garda Siochana.

Yet Supt. Kenny said he didn't want me to put up any posters. He said I would merely be drawing attention to the existence of illegal drugs! Instead, he proposed introducing undercover Gardaí into our nightclub in order to catch any "pushers".

I must pause here, to emphasise that it was Supt. Kenny who suggested using the undercover Gardaí. He swore under oath at my trial that it was I who had put forward the proposal – yet why would I tell a Garda superintendent how to perform police work? However, my wife and I welcomed the superintendent's suggestion. I agreed that my staff and I would cooperate fully with the undercover surveillance operation. No exact advice was forthcoming on how to do this, but I assumed I and my staff were to give the Gardai a free hand in their operations, to discover and arrest dealers.

The meeting appeared friendly and harmonious. The main purpose, as far as I was concerned, was to gain relief from the hostile behaviour of Sergeant McPhillips. We were also seeking guidance from Supt. Kenny on how to deal with the potential menace of illegal drugs, and any problems they might pose to our business. My wife and I placed our wholehearted trust in Supt. Kenny. We were fully convinced of his sincerity. And in turn, we felt that he accepted our own sincerity.

The following day, 10th June 1992, Supt. Kenny met with Inspector Kevin Lennon. It appears that they planned my entrapment together. Evidently, the stratagem for the surveillance operations at my nightclub was planned within twenty four hours of our original deception by Superintendent Kenny.

While I was in Mountjoy Prison, my wife reminded me of the parting comment made by Supt. Kenny as he was leaving our meeting. "Mr. Shortt, perhaps you would like to inform Sergeant McPhillips about the agreement we have reached here today regarding the use of undercover Gardaí in your nightclub." At the time, I said that I was hesitant to do this. In retrospect, it was unfortunate that I did not inform Sergeant McPhillips of the arrangement. He was one of the Gardaí who did NOT perjure himself at my trial.

Chapter Four
THE STING

I float like a butterfly, sting like a bee.
Muhammad Ali

The next Sunday when our security staff arrived for duty, I called them all into my office and told them in confidence that undercover Gardaí would be infiltrating our clientele to trap and arrest any drug dealers. I stressed that the undercovers should be given a "clear shot" at any drug dealers. I thought there might be arrests, and told my staff to remain on stand-by to render our assistance if required.

Unfortunately, I discovered far too late that it was I who was the target of the undercover Gardaí and not the dealers. So the advice I gave to my staff that night to stand back and wait proved fatal to my own interests. It was exploited in Garda evidence at my trial, and the covert assistance which I and my security staff gave to the undercover operatives was deliberately twisted by them to suit their own ends.

The surveillance operation in our nightclub started on Sunday 21st June, 1992. The two Gardaí who came in were identified by my security men, although they did not produce search warrants, nor approach me to seek my permission. We did not know their names at the time, but at my trial I learned that they were Detective Garda Noel McMahon and Garda Tina Fowley. After being told they were on the premises, I reminded my staff to give them a free hand.

(Undercover surveillance continued every night. In all, I know of six Gardaí directly involved in the operation. There may have been others who did not reveal themselves. At no time was a search warrant produced nor permission requested. These undercover Gardaí were operating, or so we thought, in accordance with the specific arrangement agreed between my wife and I and Supt. Brian Kenny. That was the reason why I never insisted on a search warrant.) *

Later on that Sunday night, Inspector Lennon entered our nightclub unannounced and in civilian clothes. An inspector of the Garda Siochana had never before called to our nightclub during a disco. I assumed his visit was to do with the meeting we had had just ten days earlier with Supt. Kenny. He spent maybe half an hour surveying the general scene. He then asked our security staff if he could have a word with me.

My wife and I invited Inspector Lennon to come upstairs where we could enjoy more privacy and quietness. In the office, the inspector drew our attention to the amount of water being drunk by our customers. He said drinking lots of water was often connected to taking the drug ecstasy. I told him that was news to me. His colleagues in the Gardaí had failed to mention this fact during the course of their drugs seminar twelve days earlier. I then explained to the inspector that we had met with his superintendent and were party to an agreement about having undercover Gardaí on our premises.

The inspector then told us of strange behaviour which he had observed in our disco earlier, and described the appearance of a man he thought was dealing in drugs. Recognising the description, I suggested a name and my wife asked Inspector Lennon why he had done nothing about it. The inspector said that it was not safe to do so, as the man was in the company of others. (During the course of my trial my defence counsel asked the inspector why he had not arrested this man and the inspector told the court: "I was alone". Perhaps Inspector Lennon had forgotten Garda McMahon and Garda Fowley, who were already on the premises? Also, a short time earlier, while the inspector was surveying the dancers, two uniformed Gardaí had actually entered the disco to check if our bars were closed. Those Gardaí had strolled right past the inspector and could have been easily co-opted to arrest that alleged dealer.)

As Inspector Lennon rose from his seat to leave our office, my wife inquired if ours was the only nightclub in his district where Garda undercover surveillance was being carried out. He said yes, we were the only one, but that similar operations would follow elsewhere. No similar Garda operations ever took place in any other nightclub in Inspector Lennon's district.

As soon as Inspector Lennon left our nightclub that night I assembled all my security men and told them about the "strange behaviour" the inspector had observed. The man described was a regular customer at our dances and we had never had any cause to suspect him of anything. However, I instructed my staff to keep a close watch on him and over the months that followed we never detected anything that could justify pulling him in for searching.

As the weeks passed by and my security staff continued to identify and steer clear of the undercover Gardaí operating in our nightclub, we began to wonder why no arrests were being made. My staff wanted to get involved themselves but I restrained them, saying it was better to let the undercovers handle matters. I warned my staff that independent action by us might be construed as interfering with official Garda operations and thereby obstructing the course of justice. I reassured my security staff that Supt. Kenny must have a clear plan of action, one that was bound to succeed and rid our nightclub of any dealers.

As it turned out, Supt. Kenny most certainly did have a clear and determined plan of action – cleverly worked out with his inspector. While my wife and I continued to operate our nightclub under the assumption that we were co-operating with the undercover officers, the Gardaí were in fact gathering evidence to prosecute me and imprison me. Supt. Kenny and Inspector Lennon had met the day following the superintendent's meeting with my wife and myself. It was at that conference that the two men obviously decided that instead of trapping the drug pushers they would instead trap me.

I was not to realise the double-cross until several months later when I was served with thirty two summonses. (At my eventual trial, I was even held responsible for drugs purchased from dealers by undercover Gardaí, and for all the tiny amounts of dealers drugs swept up off the floor of my nightclub.)

Later at my trial, Detective Garda Noel McMahon, who was a constant presence on the operation, told the court that on at least one occasion when he was buying drugs from a dealer, I was standing three to four feet away laughing at the scene. This is simply not true. Why would I laugh at the fact that this man, Noel McMahon, was buying drugs from a dealer?

(On one of the visits by Noel McMahon, my daughter Natasha sold him four pints of Smithwicks and she also sold his undercover partner Tina Fowley four or five alcoholic drinks. This was my daughter alone. God knows how many other drinks were sold to Detective McMahon).

Although I had asked my staff to leave the surveillance of our club to the undercover Gardai, on several occasions I made my own private arrests and handed dealers over to the Garda Siochana. They were taken away but no prosecutions were ever made. One in particular stands out where we did a private arrest of a man and a woman. The man had £2,500 in crumpled notes stuffed into his pockets, his socks, everywhere, the girl likewise, had £1,000. Those two people were handed personally by me to Sergeant John McPhillips. He handcuffed both of them and brought them out of our premises. Lo and behold, they arrived back an hour later – no charge.

As far as I know, the only exception to this failure to prosecute was a man whom I searched and found in possession of £480 in forged £20 notes. I handed that crook over to the Gardaí also. I was subsequently informed that a Garda superintendent took credit for the detection of that counterfeit currency.

(On one occasion in June 1993 a Belfast man was arrested by Garda Tom Conlon, after a very good piece of police work, in the vicinity of our club. He was found to be in possession of £2,500 as well as 48 Ecstasy tablets and a quantity of LSD. The file on the case was sent to the Director of Public Prosecutions, who directed that no prosecution be taken. It appeared that nothing was to interfere with the hunt of the main prey, Frank Shortt.)

*These actions of the Gardaí lacked any statutory authority. The Public Dance Halls Act, 1935, stipulated that only Garda Siochana in uniform may enter a public dance hall. The Misuse of Drugs Act 1977 states that a search warrant is necessary where Garda Siochana have grounds for suspecting that controlled drugs are in possession of a person on any premises. Article 40 of our Constitution protects the inviolability of property rights of every citizen.

Permit me here to quote the words of the Minister for Justice, Nora Owen, T.D., at Fine Gael's one-day conference on drugs in 1995 at UCD, Belfield.

"The Public Dance Halls Act of 1935 is out of step with today's Ireland. At present, the supervisory role of the Gardaí in public dance halls can only be exercised in uniform and/or with a warrant. I am reviewing this law as it clearly does not meet today's merits."

In November of that same year, during a debate on drug trafficking and drug abuse, the Minister informed the Dail that she was reviewing the powers of the Gardai to deal with the sale and misuse of drugs in pubs, dancehalls and unlicensed premises. She informed the House that at present the supervisory role of the Gardaí in public dance halls could only be exercised "in uniform".

Chapter Five

First Assault on the Point Inn, 3rd August 1992

The barbarians are coming today
What's the point of senators making laws?
Once the barbarians are here they'll do the legislating.
Constantine P. Cavafy (1863-1933)

On 3rd of August at 12:30am, I was standing at the main entrance of the Point Inn, close to the cash desk just inside the door, when a group of men wearing helmets with the visors pulled down rushed through the car park towards me, zigzagging between the cars as they came. They were dressed in what appeared to be black or very dark blue sweaters and black pants.

I was certain it was a hold-up.

The man leading the pack put his head down when he was a few feet away from me, and hit me full in the chest with his helmet. I crashed back against the desk, hurting my back. Still with their visors down, he and the other men poled right through, running past me into the Point Inn. Most of them were carrying batons, and it was at this point that I began to realise they were not criminals, but the opposite – they were Gardai.

A terrible crashing came from outside. Other Gardai (there were about sixty of them altogether) were smashing in our emergency exits, front and back, with sledgehammers. I hurried around trying to find out what was going on. The Gardai had hustled some of my young customers into our beer store and had them spread-eagled against the walls. Some of the young men I saw had their pants pulled down round their ankles and the Gardaí were shining torches up their bottoms.

On passing the ladies' toilets I heard a noise coming from inside. I went in to discover two Gardaí standing there, one male and one female. They had a young girl standing with her arms and legs spread apart. The male Garda had a flash lamp and he was pointing it down at the young girl's privates. The Ban Garda had the girl's clothes pulled up and her hand inside the girl's underwear. I openly expressed my contempt at how both Gardaí were carrying out their work, to which I was told to "Go fuck yourself".

My immediate response to this first raid was to fax a letter the following day to the Garda chief of the district, Superintendent Brian Kenny, with whom my wife and I had the agreement for combating the illegal drugs problem.

Superintendent Kenny ignored it.

On 5th August 1992, I wrote a separate letter of complaint to Padraig Flynn, TD, the Minister for Justice. His private secretary finally responded on 24th September 1992, informing me that I could make a complaint to the Garda Siochana Complaints Board. This had already been done by me. After the raid I had written to the Garda Commissioner detailing the raid and how I and my staff had completely co-operated with the Gardaí. (**See letters, Appendix 1.**)

On the morning following the first raid, the Derry Journal newspaper, which has a sizeable readership in both Northern Ireland and Donegal, carried the following heading on its front page: MAJOR RAID BY GARDAI. The article went on to quote Inspector Kevin Lennon: "The lads who took on the operation in question responded magnificently". Compare the inspector's comment with the comment – quoted in the very same newspaper – made by Lieutenant Colonel Derek Wilford after his men had shot dead fourteen innocent people during a peaceful parade in Derry. The lieutenant colonel described the behaviour of his troops as "magnificent".

Only four people were arrested out of the three hundred patrons attending our disco on that night. I'm not aware whether any of the four were in possession of illegal drugs at the time. I do know that one was the person from whom Det. Noel McMahon had purchased drugs in the nightclub. Yet none were prosecuted to a finality.

The Gardai clearly felt they had bigger fish to fry.

Following that first Garda assault, road-blocks were frequently set up by the Gardaí in order to check out the people coming and going to our nightclub. Friends of my wife and I told us that the Gardaí manning the road blocks would say they intended to continue until they had closed down the Point Inn. One of the comments heard: "We'll keep busting this place until we close it down."

Garda harassment of our business continued unabated to the total exclusion of other nightclubs in Donegal. Hounded and harassed, I had to run my legitimate business in an atmosphere of threat, intimidation and obstruction.

For months on end, young people coming to and even returning from our discos were subjected to searches – including disgraceful body searches – by the Gardaí. The community hall at a nearby village, a small village on the border just four miles from our nightclub, was opened regularly on Friday nights and hundreds of young people coming from Northern Ireland were herded into that hall and searched for illegal drugs.

In the light of the very small number of arrests following these searches, thousands of young men and women must have been wrongly detained, arrested and searched.

Surely this type of policing was in breach of the Misuse of Drugs Act, which clearly states that before members of the Garda Siochana can search a person they must have "reasonable cause to suspect that the person is in possession of a controlled drug"? It seems as if it's always open season as far as rights of young people are concerned.

The essence of the Garda campaign was to dissuade young people from attending my nightclub, thereby forcing it to close and ensure my financial ruin. In this they eventually succeeded.

Nor were these the only methods employed to shut me down.

On 21st of August, Superintendent John P. O'Connor, the new officer in charge at the Buncrana Garda Station, served notice on me that he would be objecting to the renewal of our licences at the annual licensing court in September.

I was present in the September re-licensing court that year, and no other licenses were objected to by the superintendent (notwithstanding the fact that his predecessor, Superintendent Brian Kenny, had told my wife and I that there were illegal drugs in nightclubs throughout Donegal). It appeared that Superintendent O'Connor intended to wipe out my livelihood regardless of its effect on my family's welfare. It was as if a clear decision had been made by someone in high authority (not necessarily in the Gardai) to close down our family business.

On 11th of September 1992, thirty two summonses were served on me. Thirty of those were for violations by me of the Misuse of Drug Act 1977; one for having open log fires burning and one for a supposed violation of fire regulations. This was despite all the very expensive work done the previous May in accordance with the fire officer's recommendations.

On 24th of September 1992, I was informed by the Garda Siochana Complaints Board that the Garda Commissioner had appointed Superintendent John Fitzgerald of Letterkenny Garda Station, in Donegal, to investigate the case of the Point Inn. So a high-ranking police officer in Donegal was appointed to investigate the behaviour of other officers in Donegal. It did not seem very transparent...

Yet not in my wildest dreams did I envisage what the Garda Siochana was about to do to me, my legitimate business and my family. If I had the slightest inkling, the faintest clues that this might happen I would never have placed my trust and confidence in Superintendent Brian Kenny and his undercover operation.

Chapter Six
SECOND ASSAULT ON THE POINT INN 12TH FEBRUARY 1993

On 12th February 1993, our premises were once again subjected to attack by men in dark clothes, wearing helmets with the visors pulled down, and armed with batons. The only difference? This time, there were eighty of them.

As before our main doors were standing wide open. As before, the Gardaí chose to gain entry by smashing in the doors front and back, including our two emergency fire exits, with sledgehammers. The invaders even trampled a valuable sound amplifier into the ground. (All this damage was brought to the attention of the Inspector in Charge Kevin Lennon and to his commanding officer, Superintendent John P O'Connor. No attempt was made to repair this damage or to offer compensation.)

My young customers were dragged backwards by the neck, arms and legs, and hustled outside to be searched. My own son Jalisco, the assistant manager, was himself assaulted by Sgt McPhillips. I even heard some of the Gardaí themselves urging other colleagues to show a modicum of restraint.

At the end of the raid, the Gardaí stood outside our premises and shouted to the traumatised young people: "Go home, get back across the border to Northern Ireland where you belong. This place is now closed down and will never be re-opening." Well, that says something for the Anglo Irish Agreement and for hands across the border co-operation. (I have been told by a source within the Garda in Buncrana, and the source told me that they will deny it, that the Gardaí do not want those "bastards" from Northern Ireland crossing over into the Republic.)

Following the second assault on our nightclub I was served with a further six summonses for violation of the Misuse of Drugs Act 1977. (It would be interesting to know what percentage of people who lodge complaints with the Garda Complaints Board subsequently receive harassment of one kind or another from the Gardai in their area.)

Incidentally, those second charges were held over me during all my time in prison. For instance, during the run up to my appeal the Chief State Solicitor offered to drop the second charges provided I in turn dropped my appeal. I refused to comply. I was an innocent man, and I wasn't about to pronounce myself a guilty one for the sake of not being accused of something else I hadn't done.

Shortly after the first raid, the Garda Commissioner had appointed Superintendent John Fitzgerald, of the Letterkenny Garda Station in Donegal, to investigate my complaints. As it happens, many of the Gardaí involved in that assault were from the Letterkenny area. There were also Letterkenny Garda involved in the second raid, which took place after the sergeant was appointed to the investigation.

Superintendent Fitzgerald did not interview my wife or I until July 1993, almost eleven months after I lodged my first complaint (after the first raid) and five months after the second raid. He had lunch in our home with my wife and I, and spent over seven hours writing our statements from myself, my wife, one of my sons and my daughter. I then invited him to drive the six miles to our nightclub so that he could inspect it and make recommendations.

He did, but he offered no recommendations whatsoever as regards our security, our open log fires, or the problem of illegal drugs. He took with him some private documents which I offered to loan him on condition that they be returned to me. I never received them back, despite my later requests. The progress of the investigation was so slow that I felt obliged to write the following letter, dated 7th October 1993, to the Chief Executive of the Garda Complaints Board, Sean Hurley.

Dear Mr. Hurley,

Forgive me if I got the wrong impression but it is beginning to dawn on me that the written complaints which I submitted to you over one year ago have now been released to "the scrap heap". When I called at your office on 17 February 1993 your Mr. John Grogan informed me that your board endeavoured to complete investigations on all complaints submitted to them within a three months period. How can you explain, therefore, the inordinate delay in our case?

We consider our complaints to be most serious and deserve consideration at the highest level at the earliest possible time. We are extremely disappointed that this has not been the case.

As a matter of courtesy and in the interests of fairness to all those concerned we are prepared to wait a week or so further. If, at the expiration of that time, we have not received satisfaction then we shall seek the assistance of the 'media' in order to highlight how we have been treated.

Yours sincerely,

Frank B. Shortt

Chapter Seven
THIRD ASSAULT ON THE POINT INN SEPTEMBER 30, 1994

The true blitz of terror came on the night of 30th of September, 1994, two years after the first raid. This time, two hundred Gardai came smashing in with sledgehammers, again leaving a trail of destruction in their wake. Two hundred Garda, in full riot gear. To deal with a crowd of eight hundred young people.

I was standing by the front doors when two Gardai suddenly burst past me carrying sledgehammers. I ran after them, alarmed that this time they were actually bringing the sledgehammers into the club with them. One of them dashed towards the emergency exit at the back and smashed it open from inside (all he needed to do was to press the panic bar and it would have opened). He then took a few swipes at the emergency lighting above the doors, but he couldn't reach it as he was too short. Or perhaps the sledgehammer weighed him down. At that point one of my security men made the following comment jokingly 'Frank maybe that is why there's a height restriction for the Guards'. Then the same Garda, as if frustrated by his failure, wielded his sledgehammer on his immediate surroundings, smashing all the light fittings all around him. It was nothing short of vandalism. It's a miracle that people weren't seriously injured by flying glass and timber splinters. Yet that was the sort of behaviour we had come to expect from a lot of the invading Gardaí.

The other fellow had disappeared down to the front bar where, as I discovered later, he proceeded to sledgehammer apart five of our beautiful and valuable lounge bar tables.

I sometimes wondered, as I watched these invading hordes of Gardaí invade and destroy my premises, how could they possibly spot drug dealers and drug users while they themselves were behaving in a similar way to people under the influence of drugs?

One Garda I saw was pinning a young man on the ground. He had his boot on the young lad's head, and was twisting his arm behind his back. I begged him: "Have a little bit of respect for these people, will you, please!" He told me to "Fuck off!" in a very clear, loud voice.

I also saw other young people being beaten and kicked by Gardaí. I was told by Gardaí when I tried to interfere to "get the fuck out of our way". One of our security men tried to intervene to save a young man from a bad beating and he was also assaulted right in front of my eyes by several officers. (In fairness, some of the Gardaí showed considerable courtesy and restraint. Some of those who knew me actually apologised explaining that they were merely carrying out their duties.)

Again I witnessed young men, in the beer store, with their pants dragged down and the flash lamp being shone into their hindquarters. Other young people were detained outside. When I attempted to go out after them to check how they were being treated in the darkness, I was refused the right. So I approached Superintendent John O'Connor, the officer in charge (he had also been in charge of the second raid). The superintendent's demeanour reminded me of a bee hovering over a flower, anticipating the nectar; or a cock who thought the sun had risen to hear him crow. He reminded me of Inspector Clouseau. He was dressed just like the other Gardaí, no sign of rank markings; he wore a riot helmet with the face shield pulled down. It seemed to me that he tried to be incognito. Yet, strange as it may seem, he also wore galoshes – perhaps to protect him against getting wet feet? Anyway, that was how I recognised him. Perhaps his getup was his unique way of lending an air of gravitas to the scene.

I insisted to Superintendent O'Connor that as I was not under arrest then I had a right to move around freely anywhere on my property, including the grounds. He glared at me with his cold steely gaze as though I was public enemy number one. Then, with a kind of sickly smile, he finally permitted me to go outside. There I found dozens of young people being handcuffed and flung into police wagons. One young man was taking flash photographs of the Garda behaviour and right in front of me his camera was wrenched from his grasp and smashed to smithereens under a Garda boot. I asked that young man if I could take the smashed camera as evidence. I still retain what remained of that young man's private property.

At the rear of the nightclub I came upon two police transports loaded with Gardaí. To my utter shock, these Gardaí had baseball clubs resting on their knees. It did not require much imagination to guess the purpose for which these club–wielding officers were being held in reserve.

A few weeks later, on 2nd November 1994, a newspaper article about the raid, written by well-known journalist Eamonn McCann, appeared in *Hot Press*. My first knowledge of the article came much later, when I was handed a copy of the paper by a fellow prisoner in Mountjoy Prison. Here it is in full:

> *A few weeks ago, on a Friday night, a huge force of Gardaí descended on the small Inishowen village of Quigley's Point and stormed into a disco at a popular local venue, The Point Inn. Kathy, an 18 year old who was there, recalls what happened.*
>
> *"It was terrifying. They came pounding in, in dark uniforms waving batons and roaring to 'Get Back' and 'Get up against the wall' and anybody who didn't move fast enough was thumped. Some of them had helmets on and heavy jackets. They were all excited and angry. It happened all of a sudden.*

There was a commotion and the whole place was filled with them before you had a chance to think.

"The lights went on in the middle of the confusion and the music stopped and there were chairs and tables everywhere, with people running and scrambling. A lot of people were screaming. There were bangs which sounded like shots, or I thought at that time. My first thought was that it had something to do with the paramilitaries. I dived under a seat at the side. I was shivering. The shouting kept going on and then I got up and looked around.

"They were grabbing people out of the crowd and pulling at them. People were diving in behind one another and being dragged out with arms around their necks and pushed around. I was trying to press in behind people. People were being ordered to turn out their pockets and empty their bags, but there was complete mayhem. Nobody knew what was going to happen.

"A lot of fellows were shouting 'fascists' and saying they had no right and there were roaring at them to shut up and 'Keep your fucking mouth closed'. The people who shouted were grabbed and some of them were hit. There were girls crying and hugging one another. Everyone was terrified."

A Garda spokesman said afterwards that 80 officers were involved, although the owner of the venue insisted that there were as many as 200 Gardaí inside and surrounding his premises. He said that he had been ignored when he had demanded to see a warrant, although one was shown to him later, and complained that the incident had amounted to an "assault on civil liberties". He called on local public representatives to speak out in defence of his customers and their right to attend The Point Inn without mass intimidation.

Whether it was 80 or 200 guards, it was a formidable assembly of uniformed men with the authority to deploy in a small place. Quigley's Point has a scattered population of around 400. The weekly disco is the biggest regular event in the area, drawing young people from Derry, 10 miles away and from the more immediate locality.

It goes without saying that no public representative answered the call for protests against the Garda action. The stated reason for the military scale operation had to do with "drugs". Once mention is made of "drugs" rationality and all sensitivity to civil liberties tends to go by the board.

All sorts of elements in this area who can usually be counted on to flash out instant press statements protesting when the cops come the heavy in any other context sing dumb when there's even a hint of "drugs" being involved. So hundreds of people, most of them teenagers, were physically intimidated and herded like animals and generally treated in a way which would be considered outrageous and unacceptable on any other occasion, and almost nobody spoke up for them.

Of course there are drugs available at The Point Inn discos. The operation uncovered small amounts, all of the "soft" variety, and that's been used since in the North West to argue that, on balance, the Garda operation was justified. Or that at least there's two sides to this story. Maybe the guards were a bit heavy-handed, but at the same time there was a serious problem here, something had to be done—lesser the two evils and all that. This isn't an argument which would be accepted on the basis of suspicion of any other sort of crime.

If the cops in almost any other situation corralled hundreds of people, treated them like dirt and left a sizeable number of them in tears of distress and tried to justify themselves afterwards by claiming that there had been, say, muggers among them, there'd be stern editorials in mainstream

> *newspapers, pointing out that citizens still have some rights, including the right to go freely about their business unless there's evidence that they had personally committed a crime, and that the price of retaining these rights is vigilance against the excesses of the state.*
>
> *But when its young people who are involved and there's a whisper of "drugs" the guardians of freedom all look the other way. Politically minded people yield to nobody in their militant opposition to State oppression when it's to do with some cause that they favour and sing dumb when it's mere "ravers" who they are on the receiving end.*
>
> *There's a class element in it, too. Would the Gardaí pile mob – handed into a ball at the Shelbourne and rough up anybody who stood in their way, and roar at them to keep their fucking mouths closed if they objected, and rip out the music and turf everybody unceremoniously from the premises onto St. Stephens Green in their dickey bows and stupid frocks without any suggestion of a reason to believe that the vast majority had been guilty of wrong doing of any kind?*
>
> *On what basis other than class is it deemed acceptable for young people from Donegal and Derry at a fiver-in disco in Quigley's Point to be treated any differently?*

Thus ended the Hot Press article about my nightclub, the Point Inn. Please do not make the mistake of thinking that Mr McCann was reporting on a KGB operation in Moscow, or the RUC behaviour at Drumcree. No, it was the Siege of the Point Inn, 1994. Thank you Eamonn McCann for your defence of young people and their God-given rights.

As far as the contents of the article are concerned, the reality was even worse than young Kathy stated.

The main highway between Derry and Moville was blocked two hundred meters both sides of my nightclub for three hours by a wall of squad cars directing traffic into the back roads. There were to be no witnesses. The invading force was transported into the area in Black Marias and on a number of private buses.

The bangs which Kathy took to be shots were the unnecessary sledgehammer blows smashing down the doors to our premises, and shortly afterwards those same sledgehammers being brought crashing down on tables inside our nightclub, disintegrating them into the very faces of young people sitting around them. Many of the invading hordes, those brave bold heroes, were in a highly agitated state, and seemed not accountable to anyone for the things they did or said. Our daughter Zabrina, who was only eighteen at the time, was helping out in the cloakroom on the night. She asked one of the Gardai what was going on and his response was "We'll keep busting this joint until we close it down". Every single customer was searched, including all the members of my family who were on duty (apart from myself).

Clare Murphy, reporting in the Irish Times of April 8, 2000 ("*Donegal investigation includes allegations of corruption by Gardaí*") states that "border Gardaí aren't your ordinary Gardaí. Because many of them feel they put their life on the line more often on the job, especially during the troubles. It means discipline can be a problem and they can act like cowboys."

Certainly on that night in September, our nightclub resembled the Gunfight at the O.K. Corral, with the cowboys running amok abusing our young people. Although, despite Kathy's fears, no shots were fired by anyone, I noted that several of the invading force – plain-clothed Gardaí – were carrying concealed firearms.

Why did the officers in charge feel that their men should be dressed in riot gear, some wielding sledgehammers? Perhaps the intention was to terrorise. Did they expect a riot from our young people? In reality, there was no resistance whatsoever. Inspector Pat McMorrow, of the Buncrana Garda squad, who was coordinating the third raid, remarked to my wife during the course of assault that our customers were "a very well-behaved crowd". Overhearing this remark, I immediately asked him to contrast that with the behaviour of his own men.

Surely this type of law enforcement had no place in a Western democracy at the twilight of the twentieth century. And in the tiny hamlet of Quigley's Point it was daft. The following day I once again wrote to the minister explaining the events of the night before, but to no avail.

Those riot attacks on my private property could not have taken place without a search warrant. Mr. Justice Liam McMenamin, District Court Justice in Donegal, had signed all three search warrants. At the time he was doing so I doubt very much if he anticipated just what he was unleashing against our business. Nor, I'm sure, could he have foreseen, the magnitude and ferocity of the attack which followed his sanctioning of the last warrant.

I was so incensed by the behaviour of the Gardaí that I immediately wrote by registered mail to Justice McMenamin. The following is the text of my letter:

Dear Justice McMenamin,

Last Friday night at 10.40 p.m. a very large force of uniformed and plain clothes Gardaí invaded The Point Inn, my private family company, on the strength of a Search Warrant signed by you. Several matters relating to Garda behaviour alarmed me and I think it only proper that these be brought to your attention.

(1) The first wave of Gardaí led by a sledge-hammer waving Garda rushed past me at 10.40 p.m. as I stood at the doors

of the main entrance. It was not until 10.55 p.m. that I was approached inside our nightclub by an Inspector who wished to serve the Warrant 15 minutes late.

(2) The Garda with the sledge-hammer proceeded to our two emergency exits and smashed both doors open with the hammer. These doors could have been opened very simply by gentle outward pressure on the panic bars. In addition he also smashed the "EMERGENCY EXIT" light fitting which by law we are obliged to maintain over such exits. This was wilful vandalism and totally unnecessary.

(3) That same Garda then proceeded to our public bar followed by 20/30 Gardaí where they commenced to terrorize our customers. Gardaí screamed at the top of their voices "Put your fucking hands above your heads all of you." This was roared out several times while the sledge-hammer was brought crashing down on tables smashing and damaging our property unnecessarily.

(4) During the course of the next 3 hours I, my wife and my family witnessed the civil rights and liberties of many young people being abused and trampled upon. Many young men were forced to drop their trousers to their ankles in full view of others, some of them young girls.

(5) Kevin Lennon, one of the three Garda Inspectors on the raid said to me during the course of the incursion - "this nightclub is a joint, a kip and a death trap". This is a grave insult to me and my family and such a comment is unbecoming of a Garda Officer. I will be calling for disciplinary action against this officer.

Many other disingenuous and odious incidents, too numerous to relate, also occurred. Most of the young 20/25 year old people, sons and daughters like our own children had come from Northern Ireland. Many were third level students attending universities and colleges and the vast majority were well behaved. Inspector Pat McMorrow, who was coordinating the action even remarked to my wife Sally "they are a very well behaved crowd".

Many of our customers remarked to me later on that they were astonished and indeed disappointed at the brutality of some of the Gardaí. Some of their comments "your Gardai are now behaving like the RUC." Why did the Gardaí find it necessary to behave in such a fashion?

Justice, I should be very much obliged if you would kindly inform me if the Search Warrant which you signed gave such rights and liberties to the Gardaí thus enabling them to flaunt the laws of our land.

Yours sincerely,

Frank B. Shortt
Fellow of The Institute of Chartered Accountants
Company Secretary, The Point Inn Limited

I received no answer or response of any kind to my letter.

Chapter Eight
DEATH THREATS AND ARSON

The first threat to my life came on Thursday 9th September 1993.

I received a phone call from our local parish priest, Father George McLaughlin, asking me to come at once to the parochial house in Moville. This was the priest who three years earlier had confidently proposed my name as a member of a committee of business people aimed at generating industry and jobs in the impoverished West of Ireland.

When I arrived at his house, Fr. McLaughlin was clearly distressed. He told me that he had received a phone call from a man in Derry who told him that I was going to be shot dead by the IRA. I suggested to him that it could be a crank or a hoax caller but he assured me that the threat was real – the recognised channels of communication had been used. The caller insisted that if I was prepared to close our nightclub immediately, I was to insert an article to that effect in the front page of next day's *Derry Journal*.

I immediately went to our local Garda station and reported the threat to the sergeant, who immediately passed the information on to Inspector Pat McMorrow. The inspector, together with Special Branch officers, travelled immediately to interview me. Following intense discussions and phone calls, they advised me to treat the threat as real and very serious. They suggested that it was the work of the *Direct Action Against Drugs* people, and advised me to do as demanded, and close down the Point Inn.

I followed their advice and inserted a notice of closure in the Derry Journal.

Our business remained closed up until several days before Christmas 1993. By that time we were in serious financial crisis and repayments on our £50,000 loan had fallen into arrears. I could see bankruptcy staring us in the face. So I decided to open for the Christmas season and take a chance on the other.

We were not long open when I received a phone call to come and meet some people in Derry to discuss our business. After being given assurances regarding my safety, I travelled to Derry and met with two men. My wife insisted on accompanying me. I had never seen these men before and had not the remotest idea who they were. They were well dressed, and were quite articulate and reasonably friendly at first. They talked about the effects which illegal drugs was having on young people and the damaging effect this was causing to the nationalist cause and struggle for freedom from the "Brits". They asked me to close down again and made it quite clear that if I did not comply then I must face the consequences. Those consequences were spelled out clearly to me.

Two days later we again closed our business and remained closed until the ceasefire in the following summer. With the ceasefire and the obvious goodwill that accompanied it I once again felt that it would be relatively safe to open up. We remained open for quite a few months when one morning in Derry, January 1995, I was approached in a car park by one of the men I had met previously in Derry. His new threat was forceful and brief, ending as follows: "Shortt, this time we'll teach you a lesson you'll never forget."

There was also another spate of death threats around this time, in phone calls that we never were able to trace – unlike the IRA threats the source of these new threats remained unidentified.

Several weeks later I was in Mountjoy Prison commencing a three years' sentence. My wife said, "At least you're safe in prison where nobody can get at you." Three weeks after that, the Point Inn was burnt down.

Ironically, around the same time as the threats were being made against my well-being and that of my nightclub, Inspector Patrick McMorrow, of Buncrana Garda Station, wrote to the chief fire officer of Donegal County Council suggesting that he carry out a thorough inspection of our nightclub. The inspector claimed he had reason to believe that the fire regulations were not being adhered to by the management.

Frank Kerrane, the Chief Fire officer, personally carried out a thorough inspection of our nightclub in January 1995, and expressed to me his complete satisfaction that fire regulations were being fully complied with by the Point Inn. Indeed he went on to say that our nightclub was one of the safest in Donegal.

There were many, many inspections over the period of time our nightclub was open.

First there was the team of officers from Customs and Excise, looking for liquor or cigarettes smuggled in from Northern Ireland. This would be a very serious offence for a licensed business, and would lead to our license being revoked. These officials carried out a thorough search of our premises, carefully examining kegs of beer, bottles of spirits, cartons of cigarettes and so on. They were to leave disappointed, as our company had never engaged in such illegal activity.

Next came our insurers, who shall remain nameless for obvious reasons. The insurance inspector found fault with several aspects of our nightclub such as steps, open fires, unsatisfactory locks on external doors, etc. But most of all he didn't like the lighting. Along with most nightclubs we used subdued lighting, with ultra violet lights strategically placed to display to best effect the exotic dress of our young clientele. The insurance official insisted on bright fluorescent lights being installed throughout our nightclub. This demand was utterly absurd. We could not possibly succeed with a nightclub illuminated like a lighthouse. The insurance company promptly cancelled our insurance cover, from which they had made very substantial profits for more than twenty two years. There's loyalty for you. (I strongly suspected that someone had "nobbled" a high up executive in that company.)

I immediately approached another insurance company and they were more than delighted to take over the insurance of our business. However, within two years this company also withdrew cover without giving any explanation. Of course, I really did not require an explanation.

It was then the turn of the North Western Health Board to pay us a visit. Our kitchen, food stores, beer and liquor stores, bars and toilets were thoroughly scrutinised and a detailed list of requirements prepared by the inspecting official. In all fairness to the man, he was reasonable and gave us adequate time to carry out his extensive recommendations. He returned several weeks later and expressed total satisfaction with the improvements.

Next it was the turn of the revenue commissioners. It seemed as though all of the institutions of the state had lined up in a queue to have a go at our little business. Two inspectors of taxes arrived at our business premises unannounced one Monday morning in December 1994 and asked to see our books and other records. As we maintained a proper set of books and records I had no hesitation in handing everything over to these officials. They spent practically the entire day pouring over those records and eventually asked if they could take them with them to their headquarters in Letterkenny. I did not object as there was nothing to hide. Several weeks later these records were returned to us together with an additional assessment for Value Added Tax. This new assessment was for approximately double that which we had already paid over to the revenue every two months. No explanation was given to justify the raising of this additional liability. It was my intention of course to appeal the assessment. But before I had time to do so I was lodged in Mountjoy Prison.

Chapter Nine
MY TRIAL

Trial by jury itself, instead of being a security to persons who are accused, will be a delusion, a mockery and a snare.
Lord Denham in O'Connell v The Queen, 4 September 1844

Court 14, in the Four Courts, Dublin, where I appeared on several occasions, was an insult to a vaunted Western democracy on the eve of the 21st century. It must have contravened the most fundamental and basic fire regulations laid down by law in the Fire Services Act 1981. There were no emergency exits, and no emergency lighting systems. The public address system for the judge did not function. The lawyers who were fortunate enough to have seats were squashed together elbow to elbow like canned sardines. The less lucky lawyers were forced to stand while trying to thumb through their files.

The whole scene reminded me of an old black and white film based on the show trial of Georges-Jacques Danton before a revolution tribunal in France two hundred years ago (he was guillotined moments later). If you wish to imagine some place closer to home, then think of the Carndonagh Cattle Mart on a heavy day. No offence is intended to the industrious farming community in Donegal. How do our senior counsels, with their enormous egos, countenance the intolerable conditions and environment of Court 14? Perhaps their Herculean fees neutralise such ghastly conditions.

Below the court, as I came to know later from my appeal, there was a holding cell where prisoners were also squashed together awaiting their case to be called. The conditions in that dungeon were an outrage to humanity. The stench of vomit, urine and excreta were absolutely dreadful. I was lodged there six times in all and on one of those occasions I had to endure the rotten stench for four hours. There were no windows, no ventilation and the single open toilet bowl resembled an open sewer. On one of those occasions, the two prison officers who escorted me from Mountjoy Prison for my appeal had the decency to say: "Frank, we can't send you down to that filthy hole, we'll take you to a cafe for something to eat." I can assure you, their humane gesture was very much appreciated. And further, those two decent officers did not subject me to the indignity of handcuffs, which I deeply appreciated. Court 14 and its holding dungeon are long past their sell-by date.

***

My first trial took place in October 1995 and had to be aborted after three days due to prejudicial reports in the newspapers. However, before that trial collapsed, a very important decision had been taken by the presiding judge, Justice Cyril Kelly.

During the course of the trial, Inspector Kevin Lennon gave evidence of how he secured a search warrant in Glenties from Justice Liam McMenamin. He said that he arrived at the court in Glenties after the court had gone into recess and finished for the day, so he entered the judge's private room at the rear of the court and had sworn on the Bible that he had reason to believe that drug dealing was going on in the Point Inn.

Under cross examination by Barry White, the superintendent could not tell the court where the Bible had come out of to swear the oath. You see, the clerk of the court had already left for the day, and – as my counsel said – it was unlikely that Lennon carried a Bible round in his own pocket.

Lennon also informed the court that Justice McMenamin had not questioned him one iota about the basis of his claims – in essence, never said a single word. Yet according to the Yamanoa case in the Supreme Court some years ago, the Garda seeking the search warrant must be questioned about it. My senior counsel, Barry White, argued that Justice Liam McMenamin should come before the court and give evidence regarding the conditions under which the search warrant was signed. After considerable legal argument between Mr White, the DPP and the judge, this was agreed and the judge issued instructions that Justice Liam McMenamin was to present himself before the court.

Justice McMenamin duly arrived in the Court the following morning. I and my family were sitting very close to him on that morning and we all noted that he appeared extremely agitated and nervous. Yet when Barry White called on him to take the stand, Justice Mr Cyril Kelly objected and said he had changed his mind, saying it was a precedent which he was not prepared to go along with. He rescinded the very order he insisted upon the previous day.

Justice McMenamin's obvious relief and deliverance was plain for all to see. He had been delivered from what appeared to be a very tricky situation. I don't think anybody has ever been happy about the conditions under which Inspector Kevin Lennon secured that search warrant. Why was it that at the last moment Justice McMenamin was let off the hook? What transpired overnight which had rendered Justice McMenamin's evidence dispensable, or shall I say disposable? Whatever the reason, it looked highly suspicious to me and to my family.

As a result of this the trial 'collapsed' for want of a better word and we had no time to resolve this issue but we returned to it in the second trial which took place four months later, during February 1995, in the Circuit Criminal Court in Dublin. This trial was presided over by Judge Gerard Buchanan. On the morning of the first day, I was arraigned on thirty two charges. I pleaded "not guilty" to all of these.

My two trials in Dublin's Circuit Criminal Court lasted eleven days. During that period the Director of Public Prosecutions, representing the state, brought the following state witnesses from Donegal: thirty three Garda Siochana, seven Garda sergeants, one Garda detective inspector, two Garda superintendents, one Circuit Court registrar, one District Court registrar, one District Court judge. The State witnesses from Dublin comprised: one forensic scientist, one official from the Companies Office. The forty six witnesses for the prosecution from Donegal had to be housed and fed in Dublin hotels for the duration of the trials.

At the outset of my second trial, Judge Buchanan, in a mildly vexed tone, enquired why I had had the trial transferred from Donegal to Dublin. The preliminary hearing had taken place in the new Circuit Criminal Court in Letterkenny, so the obvious place to hold the trial was in Letterkenny. The judge was clearly astonished and dismayed to be told that it was not I, but the Garda Siochana, who had brought the trial to Dublin.

Why would the Gardaí go to all the enormous expense of prosecuting the case in Dublin?

For a year or so prior to my trial, Dublin had been experiencing an unprecedented influx of illegal drugs with all the ramifications of crime associated with such a scourge. Who knows how many of the selected jury members (seven men and five women) had suffered and were continuing to suffer, in one way or another, from this awful menace? Already the spectre of vigilantism was starting to raise its ugly head. So it was not difficult to understand why the Gardaí had my trial transferred from the relatively drugs-free environment of Donegal to the capital. Indeed, friends had warned me before the trial that it would be difficult to beat the charges, given the environment in Dublin at that time. Perhaps the Gardai was also seeking media publicity for a successful drugs prosecution. Well, they certainly got that.

Following the swearing in of the jury I was asked to sit at the side of the court on my own. So much for the concept of "innocent until proven guilty". By isolating me in the "dock" the court was automatically, in my opinion, inferring my guilt. It was practically impossible for me to reach my legal team, or to discuss with them the various questionable points that arose during the course of the trial.

A further point worth mentioning was that the prosecuting team were placed immediately beside the jury, while my lawyers were on the other side of the court room. It may be a small point but it meant I felt disadvantaged from the very start.

Immediately thereafter twelve jury people were selected from approximately forty people – seven men and five women. I think it is worth mentioning here that none of the available jurors were particularly young. Older people are prone to regard some of the pastimes and entertainments associated with young people with a jaundiced eye and are likely to prejudge a case about discos and drugs. People are only human after all.

Before my trial got properly under way there was a final squabble between the judge and counsel for the DPP over the number of charges, thirty two in all. The jury were sent packing to the jury room in order that the dispute could be resolved without influencing them in any way. They were brought back eventually when it was agreed that I would face "only" thirteen charges. The judge felt that the other nineteen charges were either duplicated or of no substance and consequently they were dropped. The thirteen charges alleged that I "knowingly permitted" the sale, supply and distribution of illegal drugs in the Class C category in my nightclub, the Point Inn. These were all known as "soft" drugs – that is, there was no heroin or cocaine involved. (In fact, the estimated street value of the illegal soft drugs produced in evidence against me amounted to something under £800.)

There was no suggestion that I was directly or even indirectly involved in any illegal drugs business in my own right.

The trial finally commenced when counsel for the prosecution called witness number forty, Superintendent Brian Kenny, to the witness box.

I was under no illusion as to the importance of the superintendent's evidence. If he was to tell the truth, the whole truth and nothing but the truth as he would shortly swear to his Creator, then I had little to fear; my acquittal would be a certainty. The charges against me were laid under the Misuse of Drugs Act. If a person so charged can prove he has taken all reasonable steps to prevent the occurrence of those crimes, then it forms a valid defence in law. What more could I have done than to have written to the chief of police to help me to combat illegal drugs? What more could I have done than to offer my assistance and co-operation to his undercover team?

But if Superintendent Kenny was to violate his oath to Almighty God by relating fiction masquerading as fact then I would have a struggle to defend my plea of innocence.

The superintendent took the Holy Bible in his right hand and uttered the following words: "*I swear by almighty God that the evidence I give to this court shall be the truth, the whole truth and nothing but the truth, so help me God.*"

Later, while languishing in my prison cell I reflected often upon the voices of the many witnesses from the Garda Siochana who swore that oath on the Holy Bible. Some voices were pallid and banal; some hesitant and inaudible; some like people blessing themselves entering a church; some like a friend bidding you "good morning" while it is pouring out of the heavens. If you ever have the misfortune to be in court, just observe witnesses, particularly Gardaí, take the oath. In my trial the oath-taking seemed to be a type of charade for some members – not all – of the Gardaí in order to lend weight and credibility to their testimony.

I think the judiciary, who are the people who really know, or ought to know, what sort of evidence emanates from witness boxes, should put an end to oath-taking in our courts. Many of those oaths are sheer hypocrisy and a downright insult to God. Just how much can God take? I think truth and honesty are on the way out.

Superintendent Brian Kenny swore under oath that no arrangement or agreement had been entered into at the meeting which he had with Sally and I on June 9th 1992. Yet a clear agreement had been entered into whereby the superintendent was to introduce undercover Gardaí into the Point Inn, and I and Sally and all our staff would co-operate fully with his people.

Concerning the vital fax of the 8th June, 1992 which I had sent to Superintendent Kenny, he categorically denied five times that he ever received that fax. It was sickening to see a superintendent of the Garda Siochana give such "evidence" from a witness box.

Why was that agreement, and that fax so important?

If Superintendent Kenny had admitted to the receipt of that fax, it would be clear to all concerned that it was I who had requested the meeting – I who had taken the first step. Yet Kenny in his evidence implied to the court that it was he who had set up that meeting – that it was *he* who had come to *me*. And that was a deliberate lie.

In the lead up to my appeal, we sought discovery of various documents on the Garda file in Buncrana. The Gardaí were extremely reluctant to comply or yield them up, but finally we were supplied with a few and among them was the fax which Superintendent Kenny had denied ever having received. That fax would have to have been in the Garda file sitting in the Court for all the eight days during my trial yet not a single member of the prosecution – not the state solicitor, or counsel nor junior counsel for the prosecution, not a single member of the senior Gardaí felt it their duty to stand up and tell the court and say to the Judge, "Your Honour just a moment, here is a fax which Mr Shortt is claiming he sent".

It is inconceivable to think that Superintendent Kenny overlooked that vitally important document. Inspector Kevin Lennon, who struck me as a very thorough policeman, would surely have familiarized himself with the file prior to entry into the witness box on the third day. He also remained silent. Superintendent John P. O' Connor would surely have done likewise, but he also remained silent.

It is my belief that the prosecution team and their witnesses may not have remained silent were it not for the applause of the society which would follow a successful drugs prosecution. Yet failure to inform the court is tantamount to concealment of vital evidence which is a criminal offence in this country. Were their consciences anaesthetised, blinded by the thought of success at any cost?

A detailed account of the evidence of Superintendent Kenny appears in **Appendix 2.**

After Superintendent Kenny, Sergeant John McPhillips entered the witness box. I had never liked the sergeant's attitude towards me, but he was meticulously honest. He stated that at the checkpoint he had erected on 7th June, no-one was arrested, and no substances were seized. He also said that his inspection of the premises also turned up no evidence of drug use or dealing.

The next on the stand was Detective Garda Noel McMahon, Special Branch. This Garda was undercover in the Point Inn for at least seven successive weekends during July and August of 1992.

This witness went to great lengths to describe the types of dress which the patrons wore as if it were proof of depravity: "I noticed the people were wearing unusual dress. They did not seem to care about their demeanour. They wore track suit tops, coloured football tops, very baggy bottoms and brightly coloured baseb all boots or runners, the majority of them all wore baseball caps, different colours. The females were scantily clad, their tops consisted of swim suits, bikinis, or leotard type clothing, the bottoms were leggings or hot pants."

No doubt this was fairly typical of the scene to be found in most nightclubs throughout Ireland, but McMahon was adamant that this form of dress was unusual and "it mightn't necessarily meet with the approval of the more elderly in society or indeed the more conventional in society".

When my defence counsel tried to bring the witness into the modern world by comparing the way my clientele were dressed to Boyzone's appearances on *Top of the Pops* or on *MTV*, stripped to the waist, the witness told the court that he had no interest in Boyzone. Although at least he admitted that such type of music certainly did appeal to a high percentage of the population.

McMahon also seemed confounded by the decor and atmosphere inside the nightclub. "I noticed a large open fire burning on the left hand side of the entrance. I seen turf, I seen coal in it, it was kept going fairly brightly the whole time, there was a wall light on either side of it and the interesting thing was observing the people who would seem to be on a high, dancing with the wall lights and others looking into the flames of the fire and dancing with the flames of the fire."

The court enjoyed a good laugh at that evidence. I'm sure they must have been wondering what the detective had been "high" on himself when he observed this rare spectacle. He told the court that he only drank three or four pints of water in our nightclub each night. In fact, on one particular undercover operation, Detective McMahon consumed four pints of Smithwick Beer in our public bar prior to entering our nightclub.

McMahon also said that he "noticed at one time that it was up to seventeen to eighteen people got up on top of the tables and chairs and danced unhindered by the bouncers or Mr. Shortt. The only interference from either the bouncers or Mr. Shortt was to remove glasses that might have been broken."

Not only were patrons not permitted to stand on chairs or tables but to actually suggest that I and my security staff removed drinking glasses from between their feet simply defies belief. No properly run nightclub would condone such conduct under any circumstances and retain its insurance cover for public liability. Why did he give this extremely damaging evidence to the court? Because it was important that he portray, for the benefit of the jury, an image of gross mismanagement of the Point Inn by Frank Shortt. What else could the jury think of a proprietor who would condone such unruly behaviour in a crowded nightclub?

The witness was not quite finished with his "evidence". He told the court that on one occasion he had approached a drugs dealer, "Stocky", and asked him for two speeds, and handed him £20 very openly. "I picked my time to buy to make sure that Mr Shortt was within eye-shot of me and I was not discreet with the way I handed over the money or took back the paper wraps." The prosecutor then asked his witness how far away Mr Shortt was and he answered: "I could clearly see him; I would say five to six feet at the most."

If this was not a deliberate attempt at my entrapment by the Garda Siochana I ask you what was it? Detective Garda McMahon was at pains to tell the Court that he had behaved indiscreetly in completing the "deal" with the drugs dealer, presumably so as to provide me with the opportunity of witnessing the transaction. In reality it was highly unlikely that a dealer would risk completing a "deal" anywhere close to me or any of my security staff. Anyone I caught in possession of illegal drugs was handed over to An Garda Siochana and I have retained on file some of the precise details relating to those events. None of these dealers were ever prosecuted. At the time, I never understood why that was.

Detective Garda McMahon told the court that a week later, he once again solicited illegal drugs from "Stocky" and was sold an ecstasy tablet for £20.

Some months after my trial it was discovered that Detective Garda McMahon had been involved in a major fight in another nightclub during the early morning of that day, while he was off duty. He and his wife, in the company of other members of the Gardaí, had been drinking in the nightclub when the fight broke out. He alleged that he was knocked senseless by a "heavy blow" to the back of his head. When he came around, and got to his hands and knees, he got a "very forceful" kick to the face. He was dazed, fell down again, and was kicked in every part of his body as he lay on the floor. It is surprising, therefore, that Garda McMahon was on duty later on the same day carrying out undercover operations in my nightclub, the Point Inn.

Garda Tina Fowley and Garda Mary Finnegan had accompanied Detective Garda McMahon during undercover operations in the Point Inn. Their evidence only repeated the evidence already presented by Garda McMahon.

However, Garda Fowley – like Garda McMahon – had made two statements about events on 3rd August, the night of the first raid, and neither Gardaí had dated either statement.

When asked why she did not date her statements, Garda Fowley told the court: "I do not date statements. Because it's my statement and I know that I have made it, and I know that what's in it stands. I know it is my statement, and it is the statement that I made, I just didn't date it, I'm not in the habit of dating statements."

My counsel was also to point out to the court that Garda Fowley's second statement, relating the same incidents during the undercover operations, mentioned my name *twenty six times* when my name only appeared *three times* in her first statement. (This might imply her first statement had been rewritten with a particular aim in view.)

Quite frankly, at times I felt sorry for the young Ban Garda. She was very nervous going into the witness box. Years later, the court of Criminal Appeal would be told that Garda Tina Fowley was one of the Gardaí present in Detective McMahon's home when the Garda conspirators altered statements to ensure that I would be convicted. In my trial, it appeared to me that she had been well-tutored in advance concerning what her evidence was to be. Her tutors, of course, could not anticipate every question which my counsel would put to her. Hence, her obvious confusion when my counsel, Mr White, trapped her over the very important matter of the date on which she claimed to have prepared her first statement:

Q (from Mr White): So for all we know the statement that you say was made within a matter of days after 3rd August could have been made the night before the Book of Evidence was served on Mr. Shortt in this case?
A: (from Garda Fowley): *That is not correct, my lord.*

Q: But for all we know, I am suggesting to you that could be correct?
A: *I have said on oath that it was made within a few days.*

Q: You are saying on oath that it was made within a few days, a few days of what?
A: *Of 3rd August 1992.*

Q: What do you consider to be a few days of the 3rd August 1992?
A: *I believe in my direct evidence I said within a week.*

Q: I would suggest to you that you have to be clearly mistaken as regards the statement having been made within a week of 3rd August?
A: *That is not correct.*

Q: Would you like to reflect on that, would you like to be less dogmatic about it?
A: *That is not correct, my lord.*

Q: You are quite happy to tell me that that statement was made by 10th August?
A: *It was made within a few days of 3rd August 1992, certainly within a week.*

Q: So you are swearing on oath that that statement was made by 10th August.
A: *No, I never mentioned 10th August.*

Q: 10th August is within a week of 3rd August is it not?
A: *I said that the statement was made within a few days, certainly within a week.*

Q: Tell me then, you that are so emphatic that this statement was made by 10th August or at least 11th August, how come there is a reference in the statement to 17th August?
A: *That is correct.*

Her *"That is correct"* was typical of the incoherent answers which the court, at times, had grown to expect from Garda witnesses when they were cornered. And there was no doubt but that Garda Fowley had clearly misled the court in the same way as other Gardai had misled the court during my trial. Nevertheless, the evidence of this and other Garda witnesses helped convict me and bring about my imprisonment.

Next came the evidence of Inspector Kevin Lennon, the Garda officer who spearheaded the action against my business. It was he who met with Superintendent Kenny on the day following my decisive meeting with the Superintendent on the 9th June 1992, when both men had obviously decided upon a policy of entrapment towards me.

We now know, in the light of the evidence given by the undercover Gardaí, that the Gardaí strategy was not to nail the drug pushers as I and my wife had agreed with Superintendent Kenny, but to get me for some offence on which I could be prosecuted. This fact is now beyond doubt. My wife and I had been handed a poisoned chalice by the Gardaí. Nobody else was prosecuted as a result of the undercover operation within my private business except me. Even the two dealers from whom Detective McMahon purchased drugs escaped unscathed.

As well as buying drugs from "Stocky", the previous witness Detective Garda McMahon had also bought them from a dealer whom he nicknamed "Fringe". The last of those transactions was carried out in my nightclub on the night of the first raid, 3rd August 1992, when McMahon purchased four acid tabs and allegedly paid for them with two marked £10 sterling notes (though these were not found among Fringe's belongings later). Inspector Kevin Lennon had sent along two additional undercover Gardaí, Daniel Kelly and Paul Mannion, that night with specific instructions that "Fringe" was to be arrested as soon as he had completed the deal with Garda McMahon. Detective McMahon successfully completed the transaction and the two big strapping Gardaí immediately moved on Fringe

– but failed to arrest him, apparently because the place was crowded (although in fact it was less than hall full that night).

Instead, Fringe was arrested during the raid, along with three others, and held at Buncrana Garda Station. The charges against the other three people arrested were dropped, but not the charges against Fringe. He was to become a "pawn" in a very serious chess game.

I already knew that during the course of his interrogation by the Gardaí, several officers had suggested that they would go easy on him if he was to provide evidence against me – evidence that I was involved in drug dealing in The Point Inn. (I was informed of this by a friend, a couple of days afterwards, who warned me: "Watch out, Frank, the guards are going to nail you.")

Fortunately, Desmond discussed the matter with his father and fortunately Mr Harvey Senior knew me from years previously and would have no part or parcel in it. Apparently the father along with his son visited Inspector Lennon in Buncrana and warned him that they would have none of this nonsense against me, telling him "Mr Shortt is not into that type of thing". Nevertheless Harvey was brought to the Moville Station on drug charges, but the charges were dropped.

(Incidentally, Desmond Harvey wasn't the only arrested person encouraged to give evidence against me. A Geoffrey McClutcheon was also brought in on 20th December, and interrogated about Frank Shortt turning "a blind eye to my dealing drugs" but his written statement was later thrown out of court.)

On the fourth day of my trial, Inspector Kevin Lennon was cross-examined regarding Fringe by my senior counsel. The following is a series of questions put to the Inspector:
Q: What happened the prosecution of that particular individual?
A: *It still stands, my lord.*

Q: My instructions are that the charges against Mr (Fringe) were withdrawn?
A: *That is true, my lord, but the prosecution would still stand.*

Q: You say the charges were withdrawn?
A: *The original charges were withdrawn, my lord, but there will be new charges.*

Q: New charges were never preferred?
A: *No, my lord, because he never made himself amenable to us.*

Q: Wasn't he in Court the day that you withdrew those charges against him?
A: *I wasn't in the Court, my lord.*

Q: My instructions are that you were, in fact, in the Court, Inspector?
A: *Well, I am definite I wasn't, my lord.*

Q: My instructions are, Inspector, that you were in Court the day those charges were withdrawn.
A: *I was not in Court that day.*

Q: I am just asking him would he like to reflect on that again?
A: *Yes, my lord. I am swearing on oath I was not in Court that day.*

Q: When were those charges against Mr. (Fringe) withdrawn?
A: *I don't know the date, my lord, I wasn't there.*

Q: Inspector, you were the officer who was in charge of this particular investigation?
A: *That is correct, my lord.*

Q: Are you seriously suggesting that these charges were withdrawn unbeknownst to you?
A: *No, I am not, my lord.*

Q: Without consultation with you?
A: *Yes, there was consultation with me, my lord.*

Q: Did you have any dealings at all with Mr. (Fringe)?
A: *Very little, my lord - once in the station, that's all.*

Q: And when was that?
A: *During his period of detention.*

Q: And that was the only dealing you had with Mr. (Fringe)?
A: *And on the 8th October when I took a witness statement off him.*

Q: At the stage you took the statement off him on the 8th October 1992 had the charges against him been already withdrawn?
A: *I don't think so, my lord, no.*

Inspector Lennon went on at length to tell the court that the Garda file on Fringe was sent to the Director of Public Prosecutions and that he, Inspector Lennon, had suggested to the DPP that the charges be withdrawn. The DPP directed that Fringe be prosecuted.

Q: Were the charges against Mr. (Fringe) withdrawn after you had taken a statement from him on the 8th October 1992?
A: *I believe they were, my lord.*

Q: What was the purpose of taking the statement from him on the 8th October 1992?
A: *His father brought him forward to make the statement, my lord.*

Q: And was it on the basis that you were going to do a deal with him that if he made a statement and was prepared to come forward to swear up against Mr. Shortt, the charges against him would be dropped?
A: *I have no authority to do deals in that respect, my lord.*

Q: Whether you had the authority to do deals in this respect or not, was that the basis upon which his father brought him to you and was that the basis on which these charges were dropped against him?
A: *I did no deals, my lord.*

Q: And did you withdraw these charges against him without consulting or conferring with the Director of Public Prosecutions?
A: *I did, my lord.*

Q: Did the Director ever make any inquiries as to why these charges had never proceeded?
A: *Not that I am aware.*

The other most important aspect of the inspector's evidence concerned the search warrant that was issued to him by Judge Liam McMenamin on 31st July 1992 for the purpose of carrying out a widescale search of the Point Inn premises by sixty Garda Siochana.

Inspector Lennon, who had been granted the search warrant, told the court how he had travelled sixty five miles from the Garda Station in Buncrana to Glenties in order to get the warrant. My counsel pointed out to him that it was not necessary to travel that distance as he could easily have availed of the services of a Peace Commissioner in his own town. Legal precedent suggested that any judge issuing the warrant must themselves be satisfied that there is a reasonable ground for suspicion, and not rely on the suspicion of the member of the Garda Siochana applying for the warrant. However, when my counsel asked the inspector if he and the judge had debated over the search warrant he clearly responded: "No, he didn't ask me any questions, my lord."

So apparently Justice McMenamin signed the warrant without asking the inspector a single question.

My counsel then asked the court if it was the intention of the prosecutor to call Justice McMenamin to give evidence concerning the search warrant. The prosecutor indicated that it wasn't his intention. My counsel argued that it was unfair not to call Justice McMenamin, as not calling him would clearly prejudice my case. He put this point very strongly to the trial judge, Gerard Buchanan, but the judge's response was: "I must assume that a judge of the District Court would have exercised his jurisdiction properly."

My counsel replied: "I am sorry, my lord, no such presumption arises within the law in my respectful submission, there are no presumptions of regularity when it comes to criminal law."

Judge Buchanan came back with the comment: "I don't see how I can go behind what a District Justice said."

To which my learned counsel countered: "But he didn't say anything, that is the problem, my lord."

At that point the trial judge abruptly decided that he was ruling against us. He would entertain no further legal argument and admitted the legality of the search warrant.

Inspector Lennon was later to tell the court that the entire operation and the securing of the search warrant was so secretive and sensitive that nobody knew about it but himself. In fact, he typed up the search warrant himself. The inspector's immediate superior officer, Superintendent Brian Kenny, stated in a sworn affidavit that he was the district officer in charge and on duty in Buncrana up to the 4th August 1992, four days after the search warrant was sought, yet apparently he was not told about it. You will recall that the superintendent was the officer in charge of this investigation, the very officer whom my wife and I went to seeking help to deal with the illegal drugs in our nightclub.

In a matter so important as a warrant to search private property, I find it extraordinary that an inspector of An Garda Siochana would not consult first with his superior officer before embarking on such an important new initiative in the investigation.

The remainder of the Garda witnesses gave evidence of how they had found small samples and packages of illegal drugs on the dance floor and under seat covers on the night of the Garda raid on our nightclub 3rd August 1992. I was made to "carry the can" for these. I was held responsible for "knowingly permitting" these cigarette butts containing cannabis traces to be on our dance floor and illegal tablets under seats in our nightclub.

Prior to and during my trial I informed my legal team that, in addition to my own evidence, my wife and three of our children together with two members of our security staff were standing by to give evidence in my defence. As it happened I was to be the sole witness to give evidence in my own defence. My legal team never provided an explanation as to why no other witnesses were called, and all subsequent attempts to discover the reason got nowhere.

I entered the witness box in which I was to spend the best part of two days presenting my defence and responding to cross-examination by counsel for the prosecution. I swore the same oath as did the witnesses for the prosecution, namely: *"I swear by almighty God that the evidence that I shall give shall be the truth, the whole truth, and nothing but the truth, so help me God.*" In my case, I sincerely meant every single word of my oath. A detailed account of the evidence I gave appears in **Appendix 3**. But you already know my story.

All I said was discounted by the court. And on 1st March 1995, the presiding judge, Gerard Buchanan, made the following statement:

"I must firstly take into account the effect of those crimes on the community. I must also take into account the fact that you were warned by the Gardaí on a number of occasions before the breaches occurred. This is a privilege accorded to very few persons who come before the criminal courts. I must also take into account the cost to the state of this prosecution, which is considerate, and bearing in mind the large number of witnesses who have had to travel from Donegal to prove the case. Bearing all of these matters in mind, I will impose a sentence of three years imprisonment, on each count, to run concurrently, and a further fine of 10,000 punts."

My mouth fell open in silent disbelief. The impact from that statement was so severe that the words contained within it almost deafened me. I almost lost my balance but I stood firm against this damnation. I turned to look at my family behind me; they were rigid with shock. Security soon surrounded me and handcuffed my hands together and lead me out of the court. I didn't even have the chance to say goodbye to my family, some of whom had begun to break down crying in despair. I could see from their expressions they feared I wouldn't make it out alive.

The Gardai had won. And I, my family, my business and all the loyal staff my business employed, had lost.

ORDEAL OF FRAMED NIGHTCLUB OWNER

By DECLAN FAHY

THE wife of an innocent man jailed on the false evidence of corrupt Gardai yesterday told how the 10-year ordeal turned her family life into a living nightmare.

Sally Shortt was close to tears as she relived the moments when her husband, nightclub-owner Frank, was wrongly jailed for three years on false drug charges.

She said: "It was hard to bring up a family that had suddenly become dysfunctional. It was almost like giving us leprosy. Everybody stayed away from you."

The mother-of-five told how she once feared her innocent husband would die behind bars in Mountjoy, where he was locked up with Ireland's toughest criminals.

She said: "He was so down. Then they put him on anti-depressants.

"When he would come into the room where we would visit him, he shuffled in like an old man with a staggering gait.

"His weight had fallen down to about 11 stone and it looked as if he wouldn't make it."

Sally and the decade of trauma has left its mark on Frank.

She added: "He's changed in a number of ways. He is still on sleeping tablets. He doesn't sleep very well."

Exactly 10 years ago today, 60 Gardai, many in riot gear with sledgehammers, raided Frank's club, The Point Inn, near his home in Innishowen, Co Donegal.

Sally told Derek Davis yesterday on RTE radio that Frank, 67, had previously gone to local senior Gardai to try and clear their club of alleged drug dealers.

She said: "Frank actually went to the Chief Supt in Buncrana at the time and said I believe there are some drugs in this nightclub of ours so I would like you to help me to get rid of these drugs."

Frank was charged in 1995 with knowingly allowing drugs to be sold on his premises.

But justice was finally done when the Court of Criminal Appeal this week ruled that Frank had been framed by two senior Gardai - Superintendent Kevin Lennon and Detective Garda Noel McMahon.

The court ruled the two senior Gardai lied in court and deliberately invented and concealed vital evidence.

Sally added: "We all knew Frank didn't

He shuffled in like an old man

commit the offence. We were co-operating fully with the Gardai.

"We believed everything they told us because, after all, they are the establishment."

Frank was aged 60 when he went into prison and he and Sally's five children then ranged in age from 12 to 21.

She said: "It was awfully, awfully hard on the children.

"They got an awful hard time at school. They were bullied and sometimes didn't even want to go to school."

But the incarceration of their innocent father was not the end of the family's trauma.

Three weeks after he went into prison, The Point Inn mysteriously burnt down. Sally said: "We had just come down from visiting

TOGETHER: Frank Shortt and wife Sally at the start of his legal battle to clear his name

him in Mountjoy. I don't know who did it. We'll never know who did it."

Their eldest child, son Jalisco, was Frank's right hand man when he ran the club, but he fell apart after his father was jailed and their business was burned down.

His mother added: "He sat here in the house for nearly two years and would do nothing.

"He just couldn't bring himself to go outside the door.

"You know, it was very upsetting for me because I thought you still have to keep going on.

"But Jalisco just had this in him that life had turned against him and for a long time - even up to the time Frank came out of prison - he just wasn't interested in what was happening."

The Shortt family faced financial turmoil while Frank was in Mountjoy, forcing Sally to take on more work and cut corners where she could.

She said: "Financially we were ruined. I work as a nurse and I got a second job in a nursing home at night-time to supplement my income. I would be one of those people who keep most things to myself and I wouldn't allow the children to know that I was not able to give them what they needed.

"I would even dilute the milk when I'd be giving them their cornflakes in the morning, but then they wouldn't know that."

Frank helped out in any way he could while in prison, saving up his pound-a-day allowance to give to his family.

Sally added: "After Frank was in there for about a year or so and coming up to Christmas he sent me a letter and he said he's been on to the Governor to see if he could send me the 300 and something pounds he had saved.

"He wasn't a smoker and he didn't buy sweets. He was allowed to send us that money for Christmas. It made a lot of difference. Other people helped out - friends."

Former friends in the area deserted the family, but Sally holds no grudges.

She said: "A lot of people haven't spoken to us even though at the time I thought they were friends and I would have done a lot of things for these people.

"People just shy away from things they are not sure of. Maybe they shied away because they didn't know how to approach the situation they were in."

Sally brought the five children to see their father in prison in Dublin as often as she could.

"I would get the children up after five in the morning, leave here at six so to be in the prison for 10am.

It was almost like giving us leprosy

"We would have two hours with him in the morning and then we'd go out to have something to eat. Then we would have an hour and a half in the afternoon.

"I think the children enjoyed going in to see him. Even after he was only in a couple of weeks, his health broke down entirely and he was having awful, awful pains in his arms and so on. They did send him over to the Mater Hospital for physiotherapy.

"He spent 27 months in prison and he got 17 days release although during the time he was told if he did special courses and co-op fully with the staff, he would get a lot more for remission.

"He even entered the Listowel Poetry Competition and won first prize there for a very good poem he wrote," Sally added.

The family's fortune improved as soon as Frank was released from prison in 1998.

Frank helped to motivate Jalisco who has just got a First Class degree in Computer Science.

When Justice Adrian Hardiman ruled on Tuesday that Frank had been the victim of a miscarriage of justice, it was the end of 10 years of living hell for the family.

Sally said: "I was unable to cry, but my family around were in tears.

"It was just absolutely wonderful to think that after 10 years of fighting for justice we finally got it.

She praised her legal team saying: "If you don't get a legal team that believes in you, there is no point going looking for justice."

But Sally also said she is aware of the pain of families who have loved ones in jail - and some who are wrongfully imprisoned.

She said: "I feel sorry for people that have to suffer. I feel sorry for the families of those that are affected because of one favourable result.

"I know they are going to go through something like what I went through. They are going to go through it and I'm sorry for them."

By SHARON MILLAR

BERTIE Ahern yesterday promised that the two corrupt senior Gardai who framed

CORRUPT: McMahon and Lennon

BERTIE: JUSTICE WILL BE DONE

Frank Shortt would be investigated and brought to justice.

And top ranking Gardai will conduct an inquiry into corrupt Supt Kevin Lennon with a view to possible disciplinary action.

The Taoiseach said it was "regrettable" that a miscarriage of justice took place.

Speaking from Galway, he said: "Obviously I wish it didn't happen, but it will be fully investigated, fully examined and the people involved will be brought fully to justice."

Mr Ahern said the judgement would not undermine public faith in the Gardai.

He said: "If anything, it shows the Gardai are prepared to fully investigate if anything goes wrong."

The Court of Criminal Appeal ruled that Supt Lennon and Det Garda Noel McMahon lied in court, and invented and concealed vital evidence against nightclub owner Mr Shortt.

And the ruling means Mr Shortt can now claim massive compensation from the State.

Legal sources said yesterday that Mr Shortt could be entitled to claim huge damages because he was maliciously framed, deprived of his liberty and had his constitutional rights deliberately breached.

One source said: "His name was blackened, he was effectively deprived of a fair trial by the invention of some evidence and concealment of other evidence, and he was then deprived of his liberty when jailed.

"He would in my view be entitled to punitive damages. A very high six figure sum would not be unreasonable."

Gardai confirmed in a statement yesterday that senior Gardai will be studying the judgement and action may soon by taken.

It read: "The Commissioner takes a serious view of the content of the judgement, which will be examined by his senior officials as a priority.

"This is a comprehensive judgement and whatever action is required to be taken as a result of the examination will be done without delay."

My two sisters, constituents of the Minister for Justice, Nora Owen TD, met with her several days after my incarceration. She assured them that many other nightclub proprietors would shortly be following me into prison because of illegal drugs in their nightclubs.

This didn't happen.

Many nightclubs throughout Ireland were encountering similar problems to mine. Illegal drugs were going to enter other nightclubs – just like they entered my nightclub, whether I opposed them or not. But no other nightclub received the special treatment at the hands of the Gardai that I did. Not a single nightclub proprietor in this country, other than myself, has been jailed because of illegal drugs in his nightclub.

Chapter Ten
MOUNTJOY PRISON COMPLEX

It is said that no one truly knows a nation until one has been inside its jails. A nation should not be judged by how it treats its highest citizens, but its lowest ones.
Long Walk to Freedom – Nelson Mandela

When I was a very young boy I was told that over the gates of hell is written the following inscription: *Abandon Hope, All Ye Who Enter Here*. The gates to Mountjoy Prison should equally be inscribed: *Abandon Dignity, All Ye Who Enter Here*. Or perhaps, *Abandon Justice...*

The Mountjoy prison complex comprises two prisons: the main prison, usually referred to as the Joy, and the Training Unit. The Joy is intended to hold about four hundred and fifty prisoners. In reality it caters for six hundred and fifty prisoners or more. The overcrowding in Mountjoy has been well publicised. Prisoners are herded together indiscriminately with no separation. The young are jammed in with the old, the violent with the non-violent, the "lifers" with the thirty-day merchants, the healthy with the unhealthy. Many of the prisoners are HIV positive.

Fr. Paul St. John, one of the chaplains attached to the prison, had spent some time in Mexico, and told me that conditions in Mountjoy are comparable to anything there. "Sometimes there's a bit of an air of hopelessness about the whole thing. If it was a dogs' home there'd be protests about it." The Base, a holding section in Mountjoy, has only sufficient beds for thirty prisoners yet there can be as many as eighty prisoners sleeping there. This overcrowding leads to self-mutilation and stabbings.

Adding to the difficulties of overcrowding are the prisoners who are psychiatrically ill and ought to be hospitalised. Fourteen per cent of prisoners in Mountjoy have been inpatients in psychiatric hospitals at some stage in their lives. In 1995 there were twenty eight attempted suicides in Mountjoy. In 1996 there were sixty four attempts.

Some of the tiny cells in Mountjoy are single bed; others have twin bunk beds; some have two sets of twin bunks. When I was there, prisoners were frequently obliged to lie on mattresses thrown on the concrete floors of cells and even, in exceptional cases, made to bed down in the corridors. Mountjoy was less a prison than a human warehouse.

Inmates are restricted to the wings in which their cells are located; my area was D Wing. There I just managed to stay alive and sane for the first eleven weeks, in Cell 39. It was a single-bed dungeon, bare, dark and musty, entirely unfit for human habitation. There was not even the remotest whiff of disinfectant. The cell occupied by Kevin Barry prior to his hanging was next door. I was not alone in my cell. It was also home to a colony of clicking cockroaches and a family of mice. The previous human occupant had demanded to be evicted, as he could not tolerate the wildlife in his private hell. Yet to me, the mice were no problem. My young daughter, Azariah, loved to keep hamsters and other creatures running about at home. She did not believe in imprisoning animals. As for my other pals, the cockroaches, I used to keep scraps of food to feed them. They must have ended up the fattest beetles in the whole prison.

(Now don't think that my sanity had cracked. On the contrary, I was endeavouring to imitate the Russian psychologist Pavlov and his experiments with conditioned reflex in dogs. I hoped that in time, with patient training, my little cockroach band would win Eurovision, with a version of "Jailhouse Rock" sung by "The Joy Beetles".)

The construction of Mountjoy Prison began in 1850, just after the great famine. It may have been state-of-the-art when built, but a century and a half later it still lacked the basic facilities which even the underprivileged had come to see as an essential part of civilised existence. Today, the Joy is a Dickensian drug-infested human warehouse where human beings are hidden away from public view while serving their sentences or, worst of all, awaiting a trial.

At least the French converted the Bastille into a museum. As a museum for the display of penitentiary conditions in Victorian Ireland under British rule, Mountjoy would serve a very useful purpose. But as a place of detention in modern Ireland, the Joy is a perversion. Years ago, our foreign visitors used to expect to find the pig in the kitchen talking to the fairies. Our tourism mandarins worked hard to dispel that image. But we are still left with Mountjoy – a Victorian human zoo where people are permitted to view the inmates for a half hour, twice a week.

John Lonergan, the Chief Governor there, had the courage to admit openly on the Pat Kenny radio programme, and I quote his exact words: "Mountjoy is a hellhole; Mountjoy is a red-hot bed of drugs; Mountjoy is a disgrace, with massive over-crowding every day of the year." In 1994, Brussels sent a commission to look inside our prisons. Their report was damning and, among other things, catalogued a long list of abuses to prisoners and neglect of the facilities. To my knowledge, very little has been done to remedy that situation.

But really, why should our rulers, our modern day High Kings in Kildare Street, be in any hurry to improve matters? The vast majority of the prison population consists of the underprivileged, the unemployed, the enfeebled, the poor, the disadvantaged, the travelling people, the powerless, the low IQs and the winos. The lame ducks and driftwood of society. The High Kings consider these people disposable garbage. So why bother with them? There's no votes to be had from prisoners and precious few from their relatives.

I entered Mountjoy Prison on 1st March 1995, to commence a three-year sentence. I was brought to the admissions unit where I was made to strip naked and shower. All of my own clothing was substituted with prison apparel, which had been used by other prisoners time and time again. No real effort was made to fit me out with proper sizes. The rough denim pants and battered shirt were two sizes too big, though the shoes did fit.

Next I was photographed and fingerprinted.

During the first few weeks I was disoriented almost beyond belief, having been suddenly uprooted from the comfort of my home and family in Donegal. I had been removed from the beautiful wide open spaces, the peace and quiet of Inishowen, and imprisoned in a cold decrepit world of concrete and steel.

I suffered a sense of fatalistic submission to the system, a kind of step by step diminution of my being. "If only my friends on the New York Stock Exchange could see me now," I used to think. I had momentarily lost any inner sense of self value. I felt disillusioned, totally betrayed by the state whose laws I had respected and obeyed for almost sixty years. There was nothing to rely on but my own physical and mental strength to pull me through. I simply had to have faith in myself. But right then, I felt just as low as any human being could feel. There was only one rung lower – death. So I imagined.

Three weeks after my imprisonment, on 27th March, a prison officer came in to my cell at six in the morning and woke me up. "There's a telephone call for you." I thought this was it – somebody had died, somebody's dead. When I finally got to the phone, I didn't know what I was going to find out. When the voice came through it was Sally, my wife. She said: "Frank, the Point Inn has just been burned to the ground." So that was it.

All was gone now. Nothing. There was nothing. It was all over. We really were destroyed. I said to Sally: "Take it easy, it really is not the end of the world, take care of everybody, take care."

Three weeks after the fire we received a letter from the International Fund for Ireland. We were told the fund had cancelled the grant of £221,000, which had been approved for our state-of-the-art camping complex on our seaside lands opposite our nightclub. And as if that was not bad enough, they demanded the immediate return of the £75,000 which we had already drawn down from the grant and had already spent on the partially-completed camp site. The IFI then appointed a receiver, who immediately took over all the assets of our company including the ruins of our nightclub and the lands on which the camp park had been partially erected.

And so our titanic struggle to keep our little business alive perished amid the waves of indifference and spite. My family's livelihood lay in ruins. My wife and I did not receive a single penny from the devastation. Due to all the adverse publicity, the Point Inn had not even been insured. (We made an application under the Malicious Injury Code, but it wasn't until 1998 that the chief superintendent of the Garda Siochana issued a certificate confirming malicious arson. This delayed decision meant we couldn't even sell the Point Inn for three years.)

My wife had to return to her work as a nurse to keep things going. This surely now was rock bottom.

Then, on 5th April, I received a letter from the Institute of Chartered Accountants. The disciplinary committee of the institute stated that due to my blackened reputation, they were planning to strike me from the institute of which I had been proud to be a member for years.

Each time I thought I'd hit rock bottom, it turned out I was only hitting rocky outcrops on the way down.

Not long after, I was in my cell when I heard terrible screaming coming from the next cell. Two prisoners had burst in on this young fellow. One of those prisoners was on remand for a sexual offence (if he had been already sentenced for sexual offence he would have been in Wheatfield Prison). I tried to intervene but I couldn't; I couldn't get the door open. But anyway, the two of them burst in and they raped the young fellow. I was left at a loss of words within my cell at that point. I could not imagine hell being any worse than this.

A few days after that incident, even though it was still affecting me to some degree, I decided to sit and watch the television in the common area. I was the only one interested in the TV just then, so I flicked to a programme called "Drugs in Donegal". And suddenly, there was Inspector Kevin Lennon proudly standing in front of the burnt-out Point Inn, remarking in a derogatory fashion that the proprietor of that derelict nightclub was currently serving a prison term, in relation to the sale of illegal drugs. At that point my face flashed up on the screen. I was being humiliated in front of perhaps a million viewers. It was terrible. It was degrading. My head sunk into my hands in despair.

Chapter Eleven
MY APPEAL

As I mentioned before, I had been offered a deal from the state. If I was prepared to drop the appeal against my conviction, the state would drop a second tranche of charges against me, and in addition I would quickly be transferred to an open prison and shortly thereafter released to join my family at home.

This second list of charges related to the findings of the second and third Garda raids on the Point Inn. I had received a sentence of three years and a fine of £10,000 based on the findings of the first raid, so God only knows how severely I would be dealt with if these charges came to court. If found guilty, the sentence handed down would have been the maximum.

My family, friends and legal team encouraged me to take the offer. Perhaps they thought I wouldn't survive my sentence, or perhaps – like me – they felt utterly defeated and without hope. I thought: *Yes, yes it does look attractive, I need to get home, I need to get out of this place, my family are suffering.*

But then I thought: doing this is tantamount to an admission of guilt. And I am not guilty. So I decided not to accept the offer. I decided to remain strong in my struggle. What would the great heroes of the past do? I truly believed my soul was stronger than this.

Upon making my decision, my family life couldn't have seemed any further out of reach. I thought of my wife, who was having such a lonely time. I had photographs of Sally and the children around my cell walls, and came very close to tearing them down because they were causing me so much heartache and stress. Just looking at them brought me to tears, as I thought of the decision I had just made – a decision that only seemed to add to my family's burdens.

One of the pictures I put on the wall of my cell. It shows my wife Sally standing with our friend Alberto at his Villa in Portugal in 1982.

Another picture from the wall of my cell. This time showing my good friend Luke Kelly on one of his many visits to my house in Donegal, also my good friend Tommy Weddock is standing to his right, Kristian is on my knees, Zabrina to my left and Jalisco and Natasha to my right.' Later that night in our sitting room Luke sang one of Sally's favourites 'On Raglan Road'. Those were the good old days.

The second list of charges were never brought. (I believe the Garda Commissioner and the powers involved began to see Superintendent Lennon and Detective McMahon in their true light. Perhaps doubts had already began to creep into the credibility of these two Garda officers due to suspicious behaviour in which they were involved, including arms finds.)

So as it turned out my appeal didn't make matters worse. But it didn't make matters much better either. It took me fifteen months to get my appeal and having got it, it turned out to be a charade.

My defence team had finally – with considerable difficulty – gotten hold of the original fax which Superintendent Kenny had denied ever having received. The discovery of that fax became the main point of my appeal. If I could be shown to have sought Gardai help, rather than having had it forced upon me, I would surely be exonerated.

However, the three learned appeal court judges treated the discovery of the fax as utterly trivial and despatched it with a six-line comment: *"Whether or not the Superintendent had received the fax was a question of fact for the jury, as also was the question in general of whether they accepted Superintendent Kenny's evidence. These were issues of fact for the jury and not issues for the consideration of this court. How the jury decided them was entirely a matter for them."*

Translated, that means the jury in my original trial had already made their mind up about whether or not the superintendent had received the fax, and so there was no reason to revisit the issue. Yet the jury at my trial had not seen the actual fax; they did not have all the facts necessary to enable them to form a judgement as to whether to accept or reject the evidence of Superintendent Kenny (who said that he had never received the fax). If the prosecution had owned up and presented the fax to the court, the jury may very well have decided to reject the superintendent's denial.

One week or so prior to my appeal, Superintendent Kenny submitted an affidavit sworn on oath in which he stated: "I say and believe that the letter written by Mr. Shortt on the 8th June 1992 was not received by me prior to the meeting on the 9th June 1992. I say and believe that at no time have I disputed, whilst under cross-examination in the Circuit Criminal Court that letter was not sent. My evidence simply was that prior to the 9th June 1992, I had not received it".

But Kenny was asked four times by counsel for the defence if he had received the fax. And, four times he disclaimed any *knowledge or recollection* of that letter. While Superintendent Kenny was misleading the court, my fax was sitting in the Garda file in that court (this has since been proven by my solicitors).

In his affidavit, the superintendent is endeavouring to mislead the three judges of the Court of Appeal. I refer to questions 7a, 8a, 9a, 10a, 12a in **Appendix 2**, and the answers which the witness gave to those questions. Could the evidence of Superintendent Brian Kenny be relied upon? The evidence of that witness was instrumental in sending me to prison for three years and dooming my wife and our five children to the social wilderness.

At my appeal, the court heard how my financial means to pay the 10,000 punts fine had been destroyed. We simply could not afford to pay the fine. My business and livelihood lay in ruins. The court realised the truth of what I said and lifted the £10,000 fine. But the prison sentence stood. I felt terrible. I sat outside the court with the prison officers who had come down with me, handcuffed. Defeated once again. Back in my cell, I was unable to eat for a week.

Why was it so hard to get a fair hearing?

During my time in prison, my two sisters had two meetings with Nora Owen, the then Minister for Justice. The purpose of those meetings was to request the minister to grant me the odd weekend at home with my family, including for my twenty ninth wedding anniversary, and for the birth of my first grandchild, Reece. She refused all such requests, and told my sisters that their brother Frank was no angel. When they asked her to explain, she said that she was not at liberty to do so. I have gone to considerable length to find out what was on my file in the Department of Justice that would entitle her to make such a comment. I discovered from a certain confidential source that a note had been placed in my file from Inspector Kevin Lennon to the effect that not only was I a drug dealer, but I ran guns and arms shipments for paramilitaries and was under further investigation. Had the Gardai been planning to bring even more extraordinary charges against me? Anything seems possible.

***

During my early prison days, I looked forward with elation to my wife's visits, on her own or with the children. But every time I returned to my cell, I lapsed back into a dark depression. At one stage I said to her that it might be a better idea to cut down on the number of visits because it was not helping me. I even wondered if it was helping her or the children.

Sally detected a very serious deterioration in my health, not just physical, but mental. And gradually over the visits she began saying to me that I had to get a grip. I'll never forget her saying this: "Frank, you're not going to last in this prison, you're going to die, you must get a grip." I saw the deep look of despair on her face, like she could come to tears any moment, and it crushed me. As I told the court which cleared me of all wrongdoing: "In hindsight, my Lord, let me please say an enormous debt is due to my wife, the support from her, the sheer guts that she displayed in those dark days."

ABUSE OF POWER

This is a card I sent to my wife from Mountjoy Prison for our 29th Anniversary, 1996.

At Sally's urging, I began to "get a grip".

I remembered that people have been in much, much worse situations and have come through with flying colours. I decided I could and would overcome any difficulty.

I used to frequently teach our children that when confronted with a serious obstacle in life to practice the philosophy of "mind over matter". Now I had to do that for myself. Every morning and night I practised transcendental meditation. I used my imagination and concentration so that I became absorbed in sensory images of the past. I would relive all the good times I had with my family – like bringing Jalisco, our eldest son, fishing. Like taking holidays with the children in Spain, Portugal and Africa.

Flying to Portugal on holidays with my family. Jalisco and Natasha are in the background, Kristian is on my knees. We flew to Portugal many times and it became our favourite holiday destination to take the children.

I dredged up from my subconscious beautiful memories – the migrating whales frolicking in the surf off Big Sur, California. The hippy colonies in which Sally and I had spent time on remote beaches in Central America, with wonderful young men who were severely damaged and trying to get their lives together after serving in Vietnam. I pictured Paradise Beach, between Sierra Leone and Gambia on Africa's west coast – the most beautiful and unspoilt scene I have ever beheld. These fragments of memory and imagination helped to sustain me through the weeks of lonely days and nights.

Gunslinger of the Wild West, California 1970.

Not all prisoners had such memories to sustain them. But then they had their illegal drugs to create their own fantasies and hallucinations.

Chapter Twelve
Prison Trials and Tribulations

Men have varying strategies for coping with adversity. Mine was to insist on my rights. Many attempts were made to rob me of my dignity in prison, but I was not prepared to yield it up. Although my insistence on my rights – such as they were – certainly did not endear me to either prison governors or the prison officers.

Cell 39, Section D1, Mountjoy Prison was approximately twelve feet in length and seven in width, as measured roughly by the length of my own human feet. Within that small confinement there was a single steel bed and a small table. The concrete floor was covered with lino which had been badly burned in a fire and was coated with a thick scum of many years' detritus. The walls had the original plaster, great chunks of which had fallen off. The remaining plaster was laden with coat upon coat upon coat of paint which had flaked and peeled all over. Some despairing soul had scrawled on the wall "God is dead – signed, Fred". Underneath a different hand had written: "Fred is dead – signed, God".

The solid steel door was the original nineteenth century door with no fancy electronic locking devises or photo-electric eyes. There was one small window located nine feet above the floor, containing the original 1850 iron bars. When I first saw this small window, my only link to the outside world during the daily nineteen hours of lock-up, I began to grasp the real significance of Oscar Wilde's haunting line "that little tent of blue which prisoners call the sky".

But principally, I must not neglect to mention the "modern" toilet facility in my cell: an aluminium pot, with a lid. The diameter of the pot was only seven inches, so one had to learn to be a crack shot. Of course our political masters, I'm sure, intended this soup pot be used for "number ones". But what was a poor prisoner to do when the guards would not respond to the emergency bell for a "number two"? Which was generally the case. Forgive me for asking you to imagine yourself trying to defecate into a seven-inch wide aluminium soup pot. I weigh only twelve stone and was a good gymnast in my day. But can you imagine the contortions which a fifteen-stone man would have to undergo in order to successfully hit the target?

There were actually flush toilets, if one could persuade the guards to let you use them. Each wing of the Joy is three floors high, with corridors of archaic cells. (When I first saw this layout it reminded me of the multi-burrow rabbit warren in the wood near my home in Donegal.) The foul-smelling toilets are positioned at the end of each of these corridors. It was there that prisoners slopped out their "soup pots" and took care of their general toiletry. But the toilets weren't much better than the soup pots themselves. There was a perpetual sick odour in the air. These areas tended to be filthy with vomit, blood, faeces and urine and so prisoners were delegated to frequently hose them down. Prison officers generally steered clear of the toilets – and who could blame them. It was here that the communal syringes were swapped around, to enable prisoners shoot up heroin, and no prison officer wanted to risk being jabbed by an infected needle.

This now leads me to the point where I must inform the reader of the drug scene in Mountjoy prison. I have never even heard of a drugs culture that would in any way compare with what I witnessed in Mountjoy. One piece of research established that 31 per cent of the Prison population was using heroin intravenously. A far higher percentage (86 per cent, according to one study) smoke cannabis. Offenders can enter prison "clean" and come out addicted.

On the Rodney Rice Radio One show, Tom Hoare (the then head of the Prison Officers Association) stated: "If prison officers are turning a blind eye to illegal substances in prison it's because that's been the semi-official policy operating the prisons for the last five years. I'm saying that there's an official tolerance level for drug use in prisons; there's always been. The Department of Justice seem unwilling or unable to get their act together in relation to illegal drugs."

Again on the Rodney Rice programme, the then Minister for Justice, Nora Owen, was once asked to comment on the question of the illegal drugs crises in prisons. In her response she stated: "It is almost impossible to prevent something passing between people [visitor to prisoner] unless you put heavy glass between visitors and it is a kind of road we don't really want to go down."

Yet the Gardai had prosecuted me and the courts had sent me to prison for not preventing illegal drugs from entering my nightclub! Why, therefore, was the Minister for Justice together with the prison management not similarly prosecuted and imprisoned? Furthermore, I would like to point out that neither heroin nor cocaine were ever found on *my* premises, unlike on the heavily guarded premises of the state – Mountjoy prison.

I was inside for sixteen months before anyone mentioned hepatitis to me. It was a prisoner who advised me that I ought to be inoculated against the obvious threat from diseases arising from such filthy conditions.

I paid a visit to the prison doctor who seemed amazed that I had not already been injected against Hepatitis B. He informed me that, as a matter of procedure, I should have been inoculated immediately on entry to prison. He said he would inoculate me that evening. Two weeks later he had not done so. I decided to attend his clinic again. For two mornings in succession I placed my name on the roster to see the doctor but without success.

The governor finally got me an appointment and this time it was a different doctor. He put my name on the list for inoculation. I also mentioned to the doctor that I was continuing to suffer from shoulder injuries I had sustained in the Training Unit gym. He said that was a matter for the Training Unit doctor. He did, however, write something into a book and that evening the medical orderly gave me a painkiller. On that particular visit there were seven other prisoners in the queue to see the doctor. Prisoners were not allowed watches but I estimate that the doctor saw all eight prisoners within the space of ten minutes. The doctor's queue was the fastest moving queue in the prison.

Once again weeks passed without any sign of the inoculation. I visited the doctor again and this time it was a lady doctor. While I spoke to her about the delay in my inoculation, I was constantly being talked across by one of the four prison officers in the room. I finally asked this doctor if my consultations with her were on the basis of patient-doctor confidentiality or was she going to tolerate these interruptions. She gave me the vaccination.

***

Fortunately, I spent most of my time in prison in the Training Unit, which was constructed in 1975. This was a drugs-free facility within the Mountjoy complex. Only those prisoners who did not "do" illegal drugs, or were endeavouring to quit, could gain entry. I gained entry after spending at least 4 months in the main Prison. The atmosphere was more relaxed in this unit and the system less oppressive. And there were proper toilets, and wash-hand basins with hot and cold running water.

Each prisoner was provided with his own room, which was clean and bright. Steel bars were absent from the windows, and the doors were only locked during sleeping hours. Each room was fitted with a comfortable bed, a wardrobe, a study table and a separate table for coffee cups or the like.

Visiting arrangements were more generous and much more relaxed than the appalling visiting arrangements in the Joy. The "spy on the wall" cameras oversaw all visits to ensure no contraband was smuggled into prison. In the Joy, the food was of very poor quality and prisoners were expected to collect it and bring it back to their cells. In the Training Unit a better quality of food was served in a communal dining hall. There was little restriction on incoming or outgoing mail, and all prisoners were entitled to one telephone call per week.

The unit also had an industrial training workshop, where prisoners could learn welding, general engineering, machine tool engineering and electronics; and a school where one could study English, Irish, French, maths, photography, art or computers. Regretfully, these facilities, with the exception of computers and art, were poorly supported by the prisoners. On 19th September 1996 I wrote to the governor of the Training Unit requesting that I be granted a place on the horticulture programme. There was no response, not even a recognition that I had sent the letter. Instead, I spent twelve months, day in and day out, studying on a computer program. Under the terms of that course I was promised "generous remission" off my three-year sentence. Regardless of continuous requests to have that incentive honoured, I was denied remission.

ABUSE OF POWER

WHAT PLEADS THOU

All rise and bow your homage,
Hail Caeser who must be obeyed.
An earthly God with icon face,
Grim justice for the human race.

Wigs and cloaks and silly blokes,
All jostle for the fray.
Today they'll win or lose,
What matter, they wont pay.

With pomp and pride, deceit and guile,
They ply their age old skills.
Quoting Acts, self righteous facts,
And fancy pirouettes to thrill.

For some it is a type of show,
Some budding Hamlet or Scaramouche.
With Machiavellian counterfeit smile,
Esprit de corps Shakespearean style.

Habeas corpus, mala fides, or deceit,
Memo debit bis vexari and legalities.
Rooting and delving in their files,
Documents lost but never mind.

What pleads thou prisoner in the dock,
What awful crime brings thee here.
Have you offended man or God.
Guilty or innocent, what is your plea.

Is it murder or lustful rape,
Maybe high treason, grand larceny.
Perhaps it's hash, or stolen cash,
Or some old simple felony.

Men of grey and men of blue,
They fool the jury as a rule.
Silver tongues with oaths profane,
Don't hesitate to fix the blame.

For honest hands are rare these days.
To place upon that book of truths.
But God is watching He bleeds again,
His day will come, His will be done.

Stand to attention face your shame,
This court has found you to blame.
THREE ~~Ten~~ years of life shall be the price,
To rid you of this dreadful vice.

No more the fearful gallows beckons,
Nor reign of terror nor guillotine.
High walls of brick and cells of shame,
Conceal from all the Devil's game

Frank B. Shortt,   Mountjoy Prison   199

This is a poem I wrote using the computer facilities of the prison, I've kept a copy of it to this day.

It seemed there was really only an illusion of rehabilitation in the unit. Incoming prisoners from the drug and alcohol detox medical centre in the main prison were left to fend for themselves. If there was any after care, then I was not aware of it. However, urine samples were demanded weekly from all prisoners and if any sample revealed the presence of drugs or alcohol, that unfortunate was immediately expelled from the Training Unit back into the drugs cauldron that is the Joy.

Another unfortunate thing I would have to remark on at this point is that many of the prisoners in the Training Unit were like zombies due to the administering of the drug Methadone. This drug was administered to them by the doctor in the Training Unit to help kick their habit. I remember thinking at the time how unfortunate it was that in this day and age; an alternative route didn't exist to help drug addicts cure their drug affliction other than putting them on Methadone. Even though these prisoners were off the harder drugs, the effects of the Methadone, in my opinion, gave them the appearance as though they were high on heroin.

Chapter Thirteen
Fellowship of the Joy

I was surprised at how clean and tidy most prisoners tried to keep their cells. Of course, this was almost impossible in the main part of the prison, the Joy, because of the primitive condition of the cells. Some prisoners placed photographs of their wives, girlfriends, children and other family members around the walls of their cells so as to create some likeness of home. Others pinned up large posters of football teams, boxers, entertainers, musical groups, Bob Marley the Rasta man, grand prix racing drivers, Rasputin, and so on. And, of course, not forgetting the plentiful supply of female nudes.

One very talented and gifted prisoner in the medical unit had painted an outstanding and very fitting fresco. I was so impressed with his talent that I said to him: "Full many a flower is born to blush unseen and waste its sweetness on the desert air."

Another prisoner had practically succeeded in duplicating the botanical gardens within the tiny confines of his cell. On my first attempt to enter his jungle, a machete would have come in handy and at any moment I was expecting to be bitten by a tropical snake. When free, he was intending to start a horticulture business, and I'm sure he will make a go of it. (While I'm on that subject, I would like to spread the word and ask people to please support those "ex-cons" when they do try to make it after their release. They have done their time and paid the price.)

Television was a popular way of passing time in the evenings. Soaps like EastEnders, Coronation Street, the Bill and Emmerdale Farm were the most watched. Nature documentaries were also very popular – perhaps the unfettered freedom of the wild appeals to many humans in captivity.

The favourite films were the violent ones. It was striking that whenever there was a lull in the violence, and the characters started having an actual conversation, then the prisoners would get bored and fall to chatting among themselves or head off to the toilet.

I witnessed much actual violence while in prison. Perhaps the filthiest and most foul-mouthed occurrence I witnessed was early on in my imprisonment. I had been placed temporarily in a holding cell, one in which recent arrests or remand prisoners were usually held overnight. When I went to sleep in the cell the other two beds were empty. However, in the middle of the night the door was opened and two young and scruffy skinheads were thrown in. Both appeared to be as high as kites on drugs. I immediately became very alert as they were dangerous-looking hobos; I had to be prepared for any eventuality. For the first half hour or so they didn't appear to notice me in the dim light and they just babbled to each other incoherently or in a dialect which I now know to be exclusive to some parts of ghetto Dublin. Next morning I jotted down as much of their conversation as I could recall.

If the situation had not been fraught with danger it would have been comical; in fact it was a comedy play of sorts. Their first line of attack – when they eventually discovered where they were-was the prison officers (screws). They began to shout:

– *Fuckin' screws! Wankers with their fuckin' crew cuts! Them and their fancy fuckin' uniforms! Think the fuckin' prisin's for them! Fuckin' redneck mullah cunts the lot a' them – right, Jason?*

– *Yeah, Anton, fuckin' right. Shit happens. Bleedin' wankers, fuck all to do all day 'cept stick their pricks into somethin' for Jaysus sake – I amn't a fuckin' fool, yeh know.*

As the two continued to roar the door suddenly opened and several officers appeared and told them to behave as the other prisoner wanted to sleep. It was then they noticed me. They continued to pour insults on the officers:

– *Yis think yous is different from us runnin' around outside trying to stick your pricks into brassers. Just 'cause yous get a fuckin' ride every night – poxy mots with blow jobs.*

(I couldn't risk exploding with laughter or there would have been a riot.)

– *Fuck off yez durt birds, fuckin' scum bags. Righ', Jason?*

– *Righ', Anton.*

The officers threatened them with the "cooler" and then departed. So the Jason one turned to me:

– *Hey boss, got any gear? Any hash or other?*

I said firmly that I had nothing.

– *Where are yeh from? Eh? What are yeh in for?*

I lied to them that I was a paramilitary; it had the desired effect. (For the record, I am not a member of any paramilitary organisation, despite apparent Special Branch claims of my involvement in gun-running and drug trafficking.)

Their attitude, if you could call it that, suddenly changed.

– *Jaysus, fuckin' deadly. De ye know wha' I mean? Jaysus, Anton, another bleedin' Michael Collins. Brilliant, fuckin' brilliant. The fuckin' country's full a freedom fighters and fuckin' bleedin' hearts.*

"That's right," I snapped back at them, "and don't fucking forget it".

– Got yer Armalite with ye then? Another fuckin' anti-heroin freak – why don't ye stick to shootin' the bleedin' Brits and lay off the druggies?

– Fair play to yeh anyway. That Semtex is great stuff. Wouldn't mind shootin' up some a that for a change for fuck's sake. The only thing that's better than getting' yer hole is shootin' up or chasin' the dragon, Fuckin' brilliant, 'tiz.

With that the Jason fellow went into the toilet. He didn't bother to close the door. He dropped his pants and defecated on the floor. He then went through his faeces and removed a plastic package which he very carefully rinsed in the wash-hand basin. The package obviously contained drugs, but I was careful to ignore that scene. One of them removed his shirt and it was then I noticed the state of his arms. From slightly above the elbows, both arms bore horizontal scars, as many as twenty cuts on each arm. I understand that these were probably self-inflicted in order to draw attention to himself; a cry for help. On maybe they were full-blown suicide attempts. I was glad to see 7.30am roll in, when the two junkies were removed elsewhere.

Yes, prison is not all doom and gloom. Every Sunday morning a group of us would attend Mass in the prison gymnasium. (So you see, God is not entirely dead in our prisons.) A Sister Ignatius ("Iggy") of the Irish Sisters of Charity would play the small organ and strenuously encourage the prisoners to sing the various hymns. She was a fine venerable lady and would parade up and down through the men, many of whom were serving time for violent crime, waving her arms with great gusto, urging us on: *"One day at a time, sweet Jesus…"*

One Sunday, Brother Edmund Rice, founder of the Christian Brothers, was being canonised a saint by the Pope. Iggy thought it would be appropriate to sing in his honour: *"Mine eyes have seen the glory and the coming of the Lord; He is tramping out the vintage where the grapes of wrath are stored; Glory, glory Halleluiah…"*

By the time we got to the first Halleluiah, I couldn't sing for the laughing; most of the prisoners were already doubled up, even the "hard eggs"; the prison officers were laughing; the chief officer and assistant governor were laughing; the priest was in fits and finally even "Iggy" herself convulsed with laughter. Between trying to sing the Battle Hymn and laughing, we almost raised the roof off the gym.

Chapter Fourteen
THE PRISON GUARDS

On the first day in Cell Number 39, I went along to the Class Officer and informed her that I had no pillow. She was reading a newspaper and without lifting her head she responded: "There are none." That officer simply did not care about the prisoners' welfare, and her subsequent attitude over the following months confirmed this. Later on a fellow prisoner – the type of human being who actually had a heart – found me a pillow for my head.

On another occasion I requested an extra blanket for my bed from the governor, as I couldn't sleep due to the cold. The governor's response was: "No problem". I never got that extra blanket.

Procrastination was widespread in the jail. Prisoners' complaints were recorded on the humble "half sheet" – a meaningless document on which we were obliged to crave the most menial privilege. These were contained in Dickensian bound journals, and painstakingly written up by hand every morning at Governor's Parade, which was supposedly an opportunity for prisoners to put their requests in person to the governor of the wing.

The first morning I attended the Governor's Parade, I complained strenuously about the inhuman condition of my cell. I told the governor that my dogs lived in better kennels. His response was: "If I get you a tin of paint you can paint your cell." I told him it was no joking matter. He stated that he was not joking. I then asked him would he please come along and inspect my cell and he would then fully understand the reason for my complaint. He stated that he would do that. A week passed without his inspection, so I repeated my request. Once again, he promised to do so. In the eleven weeks which I spent in Cell 39 neither the governor nor any officer ever entered my cell.

Some prison officers make up their own rules as they go along and in general disrespect the prisoners. Others behave like robots and show a sort a mock respect for human rights.

At times, I saw prisoners grovel before their guards, and some guards indulged in sadistic cruelty. Such officers are normally referred to as "kickers". It has been known for teams of "kickers" to go to a cell in the dead of night, remove a prisoner who has been acting up or has assaulted a prison officer, bring him to a lonely place outside and kick the living daylights out of him. If he presents to the governor the following morning with black eyes or broken bones, the prison officers merely lie that other prisoners beat him up.

Of course there were many decent officers who displayed sympathy and understanding, and it was noticeable how these officers seemed to be happier in their work. But I knew of no prison officer who would let you forget that you were the prisoner and he the boss. Officers called you by your first name but you dare not reciprocate in like fashion. It was a throwback to the old British colonial days. A few times I insisted on being called my surname by prison officers. I generally received the stern, unsmiling response: "Who the hell do you think you are, *Frank?*" And I never witnessed a prison officer intervene to prevent a prisoner being abused by a fellow officer. The deeply fraternal culture of prison officers doesn't embrace prisoners. Prisoners' rights are sacrificed for the common good of the clan.

Unlike most of their civilian-clothed counterparts in the Training Unit, many of the uniformed prison officers in Mountjoy seemed to enjoy the arbitrary use of power and control. Some wore their blue-tailored shirts and blue-uniformed pants cut tight to show off their muscles and manhood, their cap tilted up at front. Crew cuts and sun-bedded complexions were common. It was all rather funny and immature if it was not so serious. Personally, I don't think that any prison officer has any business going around looking like an orang-utan and behaving as if it were all right. After all you don't see orang-utans going around looking like prison officers.

Mind you, it wasn't all tans and muscles -we had a full team of Sumo wrestlers in there as well, the prison officers with the massive bellies. Some of us used to wonder how these guys managed their love-making. The "humble ingenuous broker", my convict friend who wore out ten pairs of premium Italian shoes walking half-way around the world inside prison walls, suggested they used remote control.

The female prison officers were no better than the men. At Governor's Parade one particular morning, the governor told me that my wife had telephoned. He asked me to wait outside his door for a few moments and he would ensure that I could return her call. A female officer came up to me and insisted that I immediately leave the area, despite my explanations. A short time later the governor came looking for me, angry that I had not followed his instructions. He apologised when I explained, brought me back to that same female officer and instructed her to bring me to a telephone. After he had gone, she herself went off without doing anything about my call.

An hour later that same governor inquired of me if all was well at home. I told him that I'd still not gotten my phone call. A short time afterwards the female officer found me and brought me to an office. She closed the door behind us and started shouting at me for getting her into trouble. I threatened to report her again, and so she stopped shouting and got me my phone call. If I had been a more timid prisoner she would have carried right on. She was a typical example of those prison officers who attempt to break the spirit of prisoners in order to make them feel worthless.

I mustn't forget to mention the "free-loaders" among the officers. I'm referring, of course, not just to the vultures and hyenas who steal prisoners' food, but also to those who utilise the laundry machines, the telephone, computers, etc. And then there was the tawdry abuse of daily newspapers which are paid for by prisoners' relatives and delivered every morning to the prison gate. On many, many occasions these papers are commandeered by officers and not passed on to their respective owners until late in the evening.

The prison officers in the Training Unit did not wear uniforms and, generally speaking, were of a more congenial disposition. Of course there were several "rotten apples" there also, who merely or barely did their jobs. There were several officers who never spoke to me or bid me the time of day during all my time in the Training Unit. On one occasion my wife was left in the visitor's waiting room for one and a half hours after travelling one hundred and eighty miles from Donegal to visit me. The officer who had been designated to handle visitors on that morning had simply "forgotten" to inform me. He had also "forgotten" her. I have heard officers say to prisoners whom they wished to punish: "Wait till visiting time – pay-back time." I guess that day was payback time for me.

Prison environment can be a perfect breeding ground for bullies. However, most of the officers in the Training Unit were guilty of sins of omission rather than commission. All the outright hostility and abuse I suffered in the unit came from a single prison officer. In order to protect his rights, a privilege which he denied me, he shall remain anonymous.

People who have been held in custody will fully appreciate how easy it is to inflict subtle pain and distress on captives without even laying a finger upon them. Implied threats, cunning denial of freedom or entitlements, duplicity, neglect, omission, cold shouldering, turning a deaf ear, all are some of the endless sadistic techniques which a pitiless officer can employ against a prisoner whom he wishes to "wind up".

It would require many pages to catalogue the many painful incidents, so I will confine myself to the final letter of complaint which I made direct to the Minister for Justice in relation to this officer.

(The rules governing the conduct of prisons were laid down almost fifty years ago. I quoted two of these in my letter to the minister:

An officer shall not speak to a prisoner unnecessarily, nor shall he, by word, gesture, or demeanour, do anything which may tend to irritate any prisoner.

The Governor, in case of misconduct, may suspend any subordinate officer, and shall report the particulars without delay to the Minister.)

To the Minister for Justice,

On 26 March 1996 I lodged a written complaint regarding the behaviour of Prison Officer X towards me on several occasions. In that complaint I requested the Governor of the Training Unit to exercise the powers vested in him under Rule 126 of the Statutory Rules and Orders 1947 and report the matter to the Minister. I was subsequently assured by the Governor that this in fact had been done.
Prior to this, on 30 October 1995, I had also lodged a written four-page complaint concerning the behaviour of this same officer following a complaint by him on a P19 Form relating to alleged behaviour on my part. I was brought before the Governor to account for my behaviour and as a consequence I was issued with a warning by the Governor. At the time I protested my innocence as I was not the guilty party to the incidents.

Yesterday morning, Prison Officer X once again was the instigator of another incident when he refused to open my cell door at 9.20 a.m. following breakfast. I immediately sought the assistance of the Governor and spoke to the Assistant Governor. He dealt with the situation and issued instructions to the Chief Officer. Moments later I overheard on a walkie-talkie Prison Officer X saying to the Chief Officer: "Chief, fuck him. I don't have to take that fucking crap from him." Ten minutes or so later an assistant chief officer opened my cell door for me. Later on in the day, at 2.15 p.m. Prison Officer X once again attempted to create another incident with me but I would not 'rise' to his taunt. I had returned from exercise in the yard and was in the corridor near my door with other prisoners when officer X opened every door but passed my door. I was obliged to ask him to open my door which he did with a subtle smirk of scorn at his obvious success. At 4.30 p.m. I was called before the Governor with the Assistant Governor, the Chief Officer and Officer X also present. The Governor read over the contents of a P19 (complaint against a prisoner) submitted by Officer X and asked for my response, which I gave. I was denied my right to question the charges.

Most of what Prison Officer X stated in his P19 report simply wasn't true. He endeavoured to brand me as an aggressor and stated that it was I who initiated the incident. This officer tries to belittle prisoners and implies that they are always in the wrong and as such hides behind a bunch of lies in order to protect his behaviour. His arrogance towards prisoners, his bullying and his abuse of power are simply unacceptable to me. He consistently exhibits a lack of feeling and sensitivity towards me, and indeed towards other prisoners, and his subtle, devious and erratic attitude is intended to drive fear into the hearts of prisoners. Surely such an attitude and behaviour on the part of a prison officer is totally at variance with the general rules and regulations of prisons and is extremely damaging to the efforts made by other prison staff and management to rehabilitate prisoners. It certainly cannot make the task of other prison officers any easier and negates some of the humane and understanding attitude of most of the prison staff in the Training Unit. Management seem to be reluctant to take the side of the prisoner when incidents such as this occur and it, therefore, conveys the impression that they acquiesce to such behaviour. This may not be the intention but from where the prisoner stands it's difficult to read the situation otherwise and unfortunately the prisoner may then find his position intolerable and threatened. Certainly those prisoners who are less articulate could find themselves in a rather hopeless situation. And certainly as far as I am concerned behaviour of the type exhibited by Prison Officer X is entirely anathema to my very nature and is revolting to my professional ethos. I have never tolerated such behaviour and will not do so now. As far as the management and all other prison officers in this gaol are concerned I do not have any difficulties whatsoever and I trust that a check with the Chief Officer will bear me out in this.

In my complaint against this officer dated 26 March 1996 I expressed an opinion that Officer X was in gross violation of Rule 114 (2) of the Statutory Rules and Orders 1947 No. 320. I now reiterate that that continues to be the case. Once again I call upon the Minister to take appropriate and speedy action in relation to Prison Officer X in order to ensure that his vagarious conduct is never again visited upon me.

Minister, I would appreciate a written acknowledgement that you have had sight of this complaint.

Thank you in anticipation,

Signed: Frank B. Shortt

The foregoing letter was handed to the Governor of the prison and the following day he assured me that my letter had been passed to Nora Owen, Minister for Justice. She did not acknowledge my letter.

(The Minister did visit the Training Unit on one occasion. That was on the 29th March 1996. We knew she was coming, because we were all asked to clean and tidy up the computer room. We polished the desks and equipment in anticipation of her tour. I even wrote a letter on the word processor wishing her an enjoyable visit and congratulating her on her initiative in converting this part of the prison into a drug-free unit. However, she avoided the prisoners and chose instead to spend her time in the gymnasium with her friends, the more exalted members of society, enjoying tea, coffee and buns. The letter which I had planned to personally hand to her was, instead, given to her by the governor. She didn't answer that one either.)

On the 15th June 1996, nine days after submitting the above complaint to the minister, "payback time" arrived for me. I was returned to the harsher environment of the Joy where I languished for nearly three months, before being brought back again to the Training Unit. This was the punishment for my defiance and daring to complain.

On the morning of the 15th June, I had been told to provide a urine sample. Because the Training Unit had been designated a drug-free prison, all prisoners were obliged to sign an undertaking to provide a urine sample on request. I had already given many samples, all benign. However on this particular morning, I discovered that Officer X, the subject of my complaint, was in charge of my urine test. It struck me as being a set up, and I requested a meeting with the governor of the training unit. He was fully aware of the whole situation, yet he insisted that I would have to give the sample to that officer. He told me to go off and think about it.

I did this for several hours and then I informed him that I would comply with the contract which I had signed and I handed him a written note confirming that I was prepared to give my urine sample to any officer in the prison other than the officer in question. At this point the governor of the Training Unit became very angry, insisting that if I did not give the sample immediately then I was in violation of the contract and would be removed from the Training Unit and returned to the Joy.

I asked him to pull the contract from my file so that we could consult it. He refused. He behaved as though I had no right to question anything that happened to me in prison. It seems that I was expected to be servile and submissive at all times in the presence of such an imperious being. This assistant governor was now behaving in a most unreasonable manner. An assistant chief officer was also present and offered to get the contract. I pointed out to the assistant governor that nowhere did the contract document state that I was obliged to give my sample to a specific officer. Therefore, in offering to give my sample immediately to any officer I was complying fully with the contract.

At that stage the assistant governor became nasty; he walked to the door and called in several officers whom he obviously had instructed to be standing there. He then told me that if I did not immediately give my urine sample to the officer in question I would be transferred back to the Joy.

A rational discussion with him was just not possible. The sheer insolence of his power was sickening. It was as though he was afraid of losing. I might as well whistle down the wind. And I thought I had a way with people. He shouted at the waiting guards: "Handcuff him and take him over the wall". So I was clamped in irons with all the finesse of a Gestapo squad and immediately removed to the main prison. Photos of my family were torn roughly from the walls of my cell and, together with my personal effects, were taken away. I did not receive these again for three weeks as they had been "lost in the system". In fact, they had been carelessly and thoughtlessly flung into a black garbage bag as though they were contaminated with AIDS or the like. Bottles of after-shave lotion, whose tops had not been tightened, leached through my belongings and ruined many family photographs. It was then that I realised Mountjoy, apart from being a place of detention, was also a punishment centre.

Having drinks with two old friends Cecil (left) and Roberto (Right) in their Villa in Portugal, 1988. This was one of the pictures torn from my cell wall.

Outside Winnipeg, Manitoba in 1968. This was another of the pictures torn from my prison cell. I used to look at it sometimes just to remind myself where I had been and of the vast beauty of the world.

Eleven weeks later, presumably when the prison management felt that I was a broken man, they transferred me back to the Training Unit. It reminded me of my primary school days when teachers would punish young students for disobedience by making them stand outside the school in the cold. I guess some governors think of themselves as schoolmasters handling children. It is rather ironical and coincidental that two days before I was brought back from Mountjoy to the Training Unit the following order was posted on billboards around the unit:

Governor's Order, 27th August 1996.
All offenders may communicate by letter, on a confidential basis, with the President of the European Committee for the Prevention of Torture and Inhuman Degrading Treatment or Punishment (CPT).
Letters should be addressed to: The President, CPT, Council of Europe, F67075 Strasbourg Cedex, France.

During my period in prison I wrote to Nora Owen, the then Minister for Justice, on six occasions and did not once receive the common courtesy of a response. (My wife also wrote many times to Nora Owen. Her letters are in **Appendix 4**.)

Towards the end of my prison term, I was permitted home on weekends. On one of these weekends, four days before I was due to be permanently released, I severely strained my back lifting a heavy water pump, and was unable to get out of bed. In my opinion, my back problems began in prison due to the terrible prison mattresses. My wife immediately wrote to the governor to explain that I was incapacitated, attaching a sick note from my doctor.

The next day, I received a visit from two guards who insisted on my wife bringing them into our bedroom, where I lay spread-eagled on my bed in extreme pain. They had come to check on my condition and to deliver a fax from the assistant governor saying I would now no longer be released from prison on 2nd

May because I had broken the terms of my temporary release. Sally, very distressed, phoned the assistant governor who coldly declined an offer to have me brought back to the prison by ambulance. In the end, Sally and my oldest son, Jalisco, carried me downstairs to the car and drove me – in agony – to a chiropractor, with whose help I was able to walk with sticks two days later. Back in prison, I hobbled to the assistant governor's office. He told me he was a very busy man and to "get the fuck out" of his office. When I stood my ground and demanded he listen to me, he called two prison officers to take me away, while roaring: "You'll now serve every day of your three years."

The day of my return to prison after spending a weekend at home with my family in 1997. I carried this back injury after lifting a water pump and it didn't let up for at least 2 weeks after my return to prison.

My son Jalisco helping me out to my car to be transported back to Prison, 1997.

I had had enough. I asked the governor himself for permission to use his fax machine, which he granted provided he could read the faxes before I sent them. The faxes requested Sally to immediately apply to the High Court for a Habeus Corpus and Mandamus Review, and to gather together all the letters and evidence of the times I had been refused permission to leave the prison to attend milestone events in family life – including the fact I had not been allowed to visit her in hospital when she had major surgery.

The governor asked if I was seriously planning to go to the High Court. I said I was, and that I would bring to the attention of the court and the media all the abuses I had suffered in prison. He became very reasonable and friendly, and asked for time to contact the Minister for Justice – Nora Owen. I gave him twenty four hours and said that failing my release, Sally would immediately request my legal team to swing into action.

The following day, the governor informed me that I was free to go.

Chapter Fifteen
DIGGING THE TRENCHES

I had come to the end of my sentence in the Mountjoy gulag. Prison time, which had gone so unbearably slow, was finally close to fizzling out altogether. The eerie graveyard silence of my cell, I would hear no more. I waited patiently for the prison guard to come and give me the nod of freedom. It was within my grasp.

Ironically, a feeling of loss enveloped my soul. I believe it's a typical human character trait to become attached to anything, however miserable it makes us. Have you ever wondered why a man would go crazy if taken from the frontline of battle, even though it was driving him insane? Or why a man would object to being removed from a mental institution or a prison? He has become institutionalised – a feeling I now completely understood. I had been kept so long away from the outside world that the thought of returning to society was foreign to me. I didn't know what to expect.

The officer came to my door to release me. I was then escorted to the exit door of the Training Unit. I shook hands with Governor John Lonergan, who wished me well on my return to freedom. The doors opened and I walked out a free man.

All of a sudden a feeling of absolute liberation surged into my veins, as the rays of the sun touched my face and I closed my eyes. I looked up to the sky and smiled. I felt like a child again running around the green lands of Ballyshannon, back home in Donegal. I rose up my arms and embraced the feeling as a breeze blew through my body. I opened my eyes again and roared at the blue sky: "I'm free!".

My wife Sally was waiting nearby in the car. She got out and began to walk towards me. She was smiling. We wrapped our arms around each other and I kissed her like I hadn't kissed a lady in my entire lifetime. I was completely elated.

My beautiful wife Sally standing in our hallway in 1984.

As we drove back to Donegal, I remember feeling so many mixed emotions about the last three years. As I passed the remnants of the Point Inn, a feeling of bitterness swept over me. We stopped and got out of the car. I peered across to the old 19th century pub of mine that became the sought-after stronghold of a battle which I had lost to a relentless enemy; an enemy who had captured and destroyed it. And yet even now faced with this defeat, I got the feeling that the war wasn't over. It had only just begun.

***

I assembled my legal team and we formulated our counter-attack. The team was comprised of Eoin McGonigle (Senior Counsel), John Ward of Ward and Wall, Mr Mohan (Senior Counsel) and Desmond Murphy (Junior Counsel). My accountant, Des Peelo, also worked closely with us.

I knew I had been deliberately targeted and victimised. I was determined to fight the case and the charges right to the bitter end. I was well aware that several members of the Garda

Siochana had perjured themselves and fabricated evidence in order to get a successful conviction and also to help further their own careers and ranks within the Garda Siochana.

For instance, following the successful prosecution of my case and my imprisonment, Inspector Lennon had been promoted to the rank of Superintendent An Garda Siochana in Buncrana. In addition, I understand that he was elected Garda of the Year in County Donegal as a gesture of appreciation for his ardent devotion to duty in bringing me to heel. During the course of subsequent hearings, evidence was given that Inspector Lennon himself had specifically asked the ruling committee to award him this coveted prize. This was a man driven by insatiable ambition.

Shortly after his promotion and award he was transferred out of Buncrana to Letterkenny where he acted as chief Superintendent in the absence of the reigning Superintendent, Denis Fitzpatrick. (Yet Superintendent Lennon's shining star had reached its zenith. His reckless ambition and daredevil approach to his job, both of which came to light in evidence given to the Court of Criminal Appeal, were eventually to lead to his downfall.)

I was determined to clear my name and claim for compensation. I deployed my legal team with a rigorous strategy in order to accomplish this and to expose the perjurers within the Gardaí Siochana.

First, I needed the government to accept that I did not commit those crimes for which I was imprisoned. This case had to be won in the Court of Criminal Appeal in Dublin. This would lay the foundation on which I could build the biggest case for miscarriage of justice that would ever be heard in the Four Courts of Dublin City.

On the 20th November 2000, in the Court of Criminal Appeal, in light of the fax from my original case now being returned as evidence, along with shocking stories of corruption surfacing involving Garda Kevin Lennon and Garda Noel McMahon, the state didn't put up much of a fight and quashed my conviction without any opposition from the Director of public prosecutions, who had withdrawn 2 days earlier.

I was absolutely taken aback with excitement as the tide began to turn. For the first time in five years I began to feel victorious.

The next plan of action on the agenda was the securing of a Certificate of Miscarriage of Justice – which, if granted, would enable myself and my family to claim compensation.

This second fight culminated on the afternoon of 31st July 2002 in the court of criminal appeal in Dublin. Justice Adrian Hardiman presided over the court. A pile of new evidence began to mount up, exposing numerous discrepancies in the original case against me.

In 1999, a set of handwritten notes made by Detective McMahon throughout the period of the Garda raids had been discovered in an apartment leased by the detective. The notes were discovered by a Garda search on the apartment. These notes directly contradicted the evidence given by Detective McMahon at my trial. In the trial, McMahon had referred to "Mr Shortt" being present at an illegal drugs deal taking place in the Point Inn. In his written notes, which he had kept concealed all these years, there was no reference to myself being present on the scene. Why would McMahon keep such incriminating evidence and not burn it? I must say I had to refrain from grinning at the following suggestion by Justice Hardiman: that Lennon and McMahon's mutual suspicion of one another had led them down this dangerous path of compulsive record keeping.

There was a large number of statements prepared by Detective McMahon in the period of 1992-94. He did not disclose that there was in existence a statement which some person had obviously corrected. The statement contained detailed footnotes to be added into the statement, claiming that Frank Shortt condoned the sale of drugs in the Point Inn. The statement was to be altered to damn me at the trial. At the end of the statement the examiner had written on it 'if give evidence in Court – nasty'.

Then there was the evidence of Detective McMahon's wife, who had witnessed the above statements being fabricated in her own home. Sheenagh McMahon had stumbled on her husband Detective McMahon unexpectedly, along with Inspector Kevin Lennon and Garda Tina Foley, all in her house. She recognised her husband's notebook in Inspector Lennon's hand. While she remained in the room, she heard statements about the Point Inn being suggested and saw them being transcribed on the computer. In particular she heard Inspector Lennon dictate which portions of her husband's notebook would have to be included or excluded.

There was also additional evidence that the Gardai deliberately planted or organised others to leave drugs at the Point Inn. Detective McMahon had stated that Adrienne McGlinchey was involved with planting drugs in the Point Inn before the major raids were carried out. Detective McMahon said drugs were to be purchased in Carndonagh by Adrienne McGlinchey and then brought to the Point Inn and planted all over the club including behind the DJ box. Some of these said drugs would then have been purchased by drug dealers within the Point Inn. But this plan allegedly failed, according to McMahon, as Ms McGlinchey had got too drunk in a local bar to carry out the operation. In her stead, others did the planting. Ms McGlinchey has fervently denied all involvement with this scheme. She has reiterated that the Gardai in Donegal framed me, Frank Shortt, with their own drugs.

The state fought tooth and nail against the granting of a Certificate of Miscarriage of Justice but in the end, we won.

FRANK SHORTT

Irish Independent — Thursday, 1 August 2002 — NEWS 13

Court says gardai colluded to gain club owner's conviction

'Good to know that justice is alive and kicking'

Martha Kearns

Wrong sign, dad . . . Frank Shortt's daughter Azariah tries to restrain her dad from making the wrong victory gesture as he leaves court following yesterday's ruling which vindicated his claim that he had been wrongly accused by gardai. Right, she smiles as he gets it right.

Key factors that secured miscarriage of justice cert

The front page of The Irish Independent following the securing of my Certificate for Miscarriage of Justice, August 2002. I often laugh at this picture when I see my daughter Azariah correcting my hand gesture to the more appropriate signal.

LUAS IMPORTANT NOTICE

**Harcourt Street Closure
from: Friday - 2nd August - 7pm
to: Wednesday - 7th August - 7am**

Harcourt Street will be closed to vehicular through traffic **between Charlotte Way / Hatch St and Stokes Place from 7pm on Friday 2nd August to 7am Wednesday 7th August 2002.**

A diversion route will be posted via Charlotte Way, Hatch Street Upper, Hatch Street Lower and Leeson Street to Stephen's Green South. Hatch Street Upper will operate one way only from Harcourt Street to Earlsfort Terrace.

There will be local access only for residents and businesses to the southern end of Harcourt Street from Charlotte Way and to the northern end of Harcourt Street.

123

On 27th October 2004, the High Court in Dublin became the battleground once again for a case riddled with history and emotion on both sides. This case was effectively and unashamedly about compensation. I unreservedly believed I deserved a claim for damages. After all, I had lost everything – my businesses, my reputation, years of freedom. My family had suffered appalling losses, emotionally and financially.

I was entitled to claim damages for these breaches in my constitutional rights, along with damages for my loss of reputation, damages for deliberate and conscious abuse of statutory power, and also aggravated and exemplary damages. And I was entitled to claims in relation to conspiracy, negligence, malicious prosecution and false imprisonment.

My initial trial of 1995 was re-examined in further detail with all the new evidence which had come to light in the recent years and the fresh evidence that had been suppressed at my initial trial.

The details surrounding the fax sent to Superintendent Kenny on June 8th 1992 arose again – also the details of the phone call which I made afterwards to Superintendent Kenny to inquire if he had received the fax. This fax, denied repeatedly by Kenny, had been subsequently discovered in the Garda files. Now, ten years later, it was finally being taken seriously.

It became abundantly clear now that the Garda Siochana had been targeting the Point Inn premises throughout the early 1990s, determined to convince the community and the media, local and national, that my nightclub was being used for the sale of drugs.

Those dark nights of the Garda raids came back to haunt me as once again they were produced as evidence in the court. Again I spoke the truth, the whole truth, and nothing but the truth about those raids – so help me, God. And this time I got to speak it to a court that was prepared to listen.

The allegations of Mrs Sheenagh McMahon, the estranged wife of Detective Garda Noel McMahon, were also heard again. He had personally told her himself that he had perjured himself at my trial. He admitted to the perjury because he was enraged at the fact that Superintendent Kevin Lennon had received a divisional policing award upon my imprisonment.

Additionally, the grounds on which the Certificate for Miscarriage of Justice was granted was re-examined. Mr Justice Finnegan heard how there was effectively three matters which aided the granting of the certificate. These were the fabrication of evidence in relation to statements, the allegation of perjury by the witnesses, and the planting of evidence by one of the witnesses.

Insofar as there had been a plan by the Garda Siochana to close or to damage the Point Inn limited and those who ran it, as of 1st March of 1995 their plan had completely and utterly succeeded.

The court heard that I effectively had become a destroyed person, not only internally to myself but also externally to the community. The court also heard how my family became relations of "that bastard Frank Shortt, the drug dealer" and how they were all shunned in the local community in Donegal. To be a person, at that time approximately sixty years of age, being photographed leaving the court in handcuffs, to have to witness my distraught family as I was taken away and to be placed in Mountjoy and also to read in every newspaper in the country the sentence and the details of why I was sentenced – these things had had a devastating effect upon me and my family.

4 THE IRISH TIMES, Thursday, August 1, 2002

THE SHORTT CASE

Shortt case gardai 'invented' evidence

By Mary Carolan

THE "deliberate suppression" of evidence by two senior gardai entitled Co Donegal nightclub owner Frank Shortt to a certificate declaring a miscarriage of justice arising from his conviction for knowingly allowing the sale of drugs at his club, the Point Inn, Inishowen, the Court of Criminal Appeal held yesterday. The court also found that certain evidence was deliberately "invented" by both gardai.

The three-judge court ruled that there was a miscarriage of justice on the grounds of newly-discovered facts – the deliberate suppression of material by Det Garda Noel McMahon and Supt Kevin Lennon.

Mr Shortt served three years in prison arising from his 1995 conviction.

It was set aside by the CCA in November 2000, with no opposition from the DPP, after certain allegations were made in the report of the internal Carty Garda inquiry into alleged corruption by gardai in Co Donegal.

In granting the certificate, which enables Mr Shortt to sue for compensation, Mr Justice Hardiman, presiding, sitting with Mr Justice O'Donovan and Mr Justice O'Higgins, said that the court had focused principally on the "transformation" which occurred in the evidence of Det McMahon, the principal witness against Mr Shortt, about September 1994, prior to Mr Shortt's trial.

"We have concluded that particular evidence was invented at that time to address certain serious weaknesses in the case against him which became apparent on or shortly after September 1st, 1994. To avoid this invention being discovered, certain essential documents were concealed at the trial."

Those documents comprised Det McMahon's original notes and a further statement of Det McMahon's on which notes were written by his superior – Supt Lennon (then an inspector) – "with a view to suggesting that he create an expanded version of his original statement of evidence".

The latter document was concealed even when a direct question was asked which, if truthfully and completely answered, would have involved its disclosure, the court found. "We find that this invention and concealment were conscious and deliberate acts". It held that Det McMahon and Supt Lennon had deliberately concealed these documents and were fully conscious of their importance to Mr Shortt's defence.

The court said that the more probable version of how new material came to feature in Det McMahon's evidence to the trial was that, having read an Advice on Proofs document from counsel, which highlighted weaknesses in the case, the detective produced a further statement which was still unsatisfactory from Supt Lennon's point of view and which still made no mention of the specific allegation about Mr Shortt. That led to Det McMahon meeting with Supt Lennon. This meeting, the court held, was the genesis of the "new and highly-specific allegations against Shortt".

The court said that, "very regrettably", it had to conclude that it was more probable that the additions to Det McMahon's statement – signified by phrases such as "Where is Shortt – say he was nearby" – were inspired by Supt Lennon and acquiesced in by Det McMahon. The court was driven to the conclusion that Supt Lennon had determined to strengthen the case against Mr Shortt to the extent necessary to make a conviction likely.

The court also accepted evidence from Ms Sheenagh McMahon that Det McMahon, her estranged husband, had told her he had perjured himself during the trial of Mr Shortt. Ms McMahon had impressed the court as "a truthful and generally accurate witness". It found her evidence consistent with other evidence, including the "pattern of change" in the statements of evidence and two "wholly extraordinary" draft letters, one by Det McMahon and the second by Supt Lennon, described as "letters of satisfaction".

"We reject the explanation of these documents given by the gardai mentioned." The court believed that the letters of satisfaction, which included an assertion by Det McMahon (on Supt Lennon's draft) that he [Det McMahon] had never known Supt Lennon to be inv ved in any unlawful activity "demonstrate that allegations within the gardai about the Point Inn operation were a matter of grave concern to Supt Lennon almost four years after the operation has concluded". Neither Det McMahon nor Supt Lennon had advanced any credible explanation of these letters.

The content of the letters was "so unusual and dramatic" – amounting to a garda assuring a superintendent or another member that he had never known the superintendent to act illegally – that it was not possible to accept that either Det McMahon or Supt Lennon could simply have forgotten what allegations of illegal acts led to the writing of the respective drafts.

While the court's non-acceptance of the evidence of the gardai on those letters did not conclusively demonstrate that the allegations of illegal activities related to the Point Inn, the court was of the opinion, as a matter of probability, that it did relate to the Point Inn at least in part. It was possible to say that the precise nature of the concern which the Point Inn operation presented to Supt Lennon in 1996 related to allegations of illegal activities participated in or authorised by him in connection with that operation.

Given its findings on the above matters, the court said it was unnecessary to consider certain other evidence given at the hearing. It also said that while certain documents were overlooked and sometimes produced later in the day, it was satisfied that no documents were deliberately concealed by either the DPP or the gardai conducting the Carty inquiry into alleged corruption by gardai in Co Donegal. It praised the work done by Mr Brian McCreary, solicitor for the DPP, and Mr John Ward, solicitor for Mr Shortt.

Det McMahon and Supt Lennon, both formerly attached to Buncrana Garda station, were involved in Operation Spider, an undercover Garda operation into alleged drug-dealing at the Point Inn in 1992. Det McMahon was the chief prosecution witness at Mr Shortt's trial, while Supt Lennon, then an inspector, headed the investigation.

During the 16-day hearing of Mr Shortt's application for a certificate, allegations were made by Ms Sheenagh McMahon that her estranged husband told her he perjured himself at Mr Shortt's trial and did so in order to get Supt Lennon promoted.

Ms Adrienne McGlinchey also made allegations that Mr Shortt was framed by the gardai. She made further claims that Det McMahon and Supt Lennon were involved in planting explosives at locations in Co Donegal to be found subsequently by gardai.

These claims were denied by both gardai.

In its judgment, the court noted that the case against Mr Shortt was very weak in September 1994, with senior counsel for the DPP noting, having read the Book of Evidence, that Mr Shortt was not mentioned as being present when drugs were changing hands and that Det McMahon's then statement seemed to indicate that the Shortts did not know what was going on in their premises.

The court noted that, in his evidence at Mr Shortt's trial, Det McMahon was the principal prosecution witness and had named or described persons from whom he purchased drugs at the Point Inn and had said he took considerable pains to ensure certain of the transactions were visible to Mr Shortt.

The court also noted that Mr Shortt had contended at the trial that he had reached an agreement with Supt Kenny that undercover gardai would be placed at the Point Inn. Supt Kenny had agreed in evidence that Mr Shortt had suggested this to him, but the superintendent had said he made no "firm decision" to put gardai in on Mr Shortt's suggestion.

Mr Shortt had said at the trial that he did see suspicious transactions, but knew not to interfere "because I knew they were gardai acting under cover".

The credibility of this alleged arrangement, and of the defence which Mr Shortt built on it, would be severely compromised if Det McMahon's evidence was accepted, the court said. However, if Mr Shortt's defence was accepted, there would be no case against him.

The court held that Det McMahon's evidence to the trial was severely questioned and observed that his notes lacked the detail which was a strong feature of the evidence he gave. At no stage did the detective disclose a quite separate set of notes or a draft second statement of evidence annotated by Supt Lennon.

It seemed that the existence of a whole sequence of notes and other material was forgotten or concealed by Det McMahon at the trial, the court held.

It found that there was no basis in Det McMahon's contemporary written notes to support the specific allegations against Mr Shortt which the detective had produced after receiving the Advice on Proofs document (setting out what would be required to secure a conviction) and after meeting with Supt Lennon.

The court found it most unlikely that such an experienced police officer would have failed to note, when making notes within hours of its occurring, such a dramatic piece of evidence as his assertion that Mr Shortt was present when the detective bought drugs at the Point.

The court also set out in table form a comparative analysis of Det McMahon's various records, including his annotated statement, relating to the surveillance operation at the Point, and highlighted inconsistencies between these.

Dealing with Ms McGlinchey's evidence, the court found that there were conflicts surrounding this. However, it noted, it was indisputable that had Ms McGlinchey not made certain allegations to the Carty inquiry, the process which led to the discovery of other unquestionably significant facts relating to Mr Shortt's conviction would not have started.

Matters unrelated to Ms McGlinchey established a miscarriage of justice and made it unnecessary to record any findings on her evidence.

Supt Kevin Lennon (left) and Det Garda Noel McMahon, who were yesterday found by the Court of Criminal Appeal to have suppressed evidence in the case against Mr Frank Shortt, a Donegal nightclub owner. Photographs: Ronan Quinlan/Collins

The new material that led to court's decision

By Mary Carolan

THE newly discovered material which formed the basis of the court's decision consisted of:

1) Allegations by Ms Sheenagh McMahon, especially that Det McMahon told her he perjured himself during Mr Shortt's trial;

2) The evidence of Ms Adrienne McGlinchey that she was given money to buy drugs and asked by Det McMahon to plant the drugs in the Point Inn. She told the court she agreed to plant drugs but failed to do so and that she was later told by Det McMahon that others had planted them. The Carty inquiry also recorded Ms McGlinchey as alleging she was asked to plant drugs, with the vital difference that the Carty team stated she told them she *had* planted the drugs. The memo with that allegation was not signed by her.

3) A remark by Det McMahon, during interviews with the Carty team, that Ms McGlinchey was "never in the Point Inn, she was supposed to go there but she never went".

4) Evidence by Det McMahon to the court in which he conceded for the first time Ms McGlinchey was aware of the Point Inn operation before the raid.

5) Material taken from Det McMahon's home during a raid by the Carty team in September 1999. This included a number of loose sheets of paper in Det McMahon's handwriting dealing with events at the Point Inn from June to September 1992, a draft of Det McMahon's second statement with annotations by Supt Lennon and an Advice on Proofs document outlining concerns about deficiencies in the case against Mr Shortt.

6) The "letter of satisfaction", a document in two forms. The first was a typewritten letter by Det McMahon while the second was a handwritten draft by Supt Lennon. In both forms, which appeared to date from 1996, the nature of the contents was a "strong endorsement" of Supt Lennon by Det McMahon.

7) A list in Det McMahon's handwriting which appeared to be a list of concerns which may have prompted the writing of the "letter of satisfaction". The fifth item said: "Point Inn etc etc".

8) The discovery of two premarked £10 sterling notes in the possession of an alleged drug dealer. The notes were found in the property of the alleged dealer after this was searched, at Det McMahon's request, on the afternoon of August 3rd, 1992, hours after an early-morning Garda raid on the Point Inn. But when the dealer was searched on the night of the raid, no such notes were then found.

9) An allegation by Sheenagh McMahon that she saw Det McMahon, Supt Lennon and two other gardai in a room of her home preparing a statement for Mr Shortt's trial. She alleged Supt Lennon was reading from a notebook of her husband's and was giving instructions on what to include and exclude.

10) A four-page document in Det McMahon's handwriting with the words: "Point Inn – perjury – set up – advice on proofs – Kevin Lennon had my notebook".

11) Notes in Det McMahon's handwriting. The words "Shortt-merit award – tout" were all on the same line and appeared to be linked, the court said.

'It's good to know justice is alive and kicking still in this country'

By Paul Cullen

"THIS is absolutely wonderful. It's good to know that justice is alive and kicking still in this country," were Mr Frank Shortt's first words as he emerged yesterday from the Four Courts to a ring of television cameras and microphones.

The Court of Criminal Appeal had just taken five minutes to deliver a historic judgment that declared a miscarriage of justice in the case of the former nightclub owner from Co Donegal.

It was a quick end to a long legal battle for Mr Shortt and his family, which included 16 days of evidence last month, a series of trials, a three-year spell in jail and a later quashing of the conviction that led to his imprisonment.

Mr Shortt insisted he wasn't bitter about his experiences with the gardai and in jail. "You can't live with bitterness," he reflected. "It's over with now. I don't even feel bitter about the people who put me into prison.

"My wife Sally, myself and my children suffered extensively at the hands of the State over a period of 8 to 10 years, but it's all over with now and we hope to get down to living a quiet life."

His voice quivering and his hands trembling, he recalled he had written a book about his experiences while in prison. "Another chapter will have to be added to it now."

As for the gardai, Mr Shortt felt they were just "doing a job. Just because there were one or two rotten apples doesn't mean you can condemn the whole force.

"We're lucky in this country that we do have, by and large, a pretty decent bunch of policemen."

But asked whether he was happy with the action taken by the force to root out the "bad apples", he replied with an emphatic "No".

"I don't believe they have done their job properly. It's up to the DPP and the Minister for Justice to take the appropriate action against the people whom they perceive were the cause of all this trouble. After all, what was done by a handful of gardai didn't do the force any good."

A reporter wanted to know what he thought of the Garda Síochána now. "Well, he won't be joining them anyway," his wife Sally joked.

Asked about his possible involvement in the Morris Tribunal, which is enquiring into complaints against some gardai in the Donegal Division, Mr Shortt said he'd "had enough" of court hearings for now. It was a matter for Mr Justice Morris to decide, he added.

Mr Shortt's lawyers will now prepare a compensation claim. As for their client, he delivered a final word of praise for the "magnificent" judges who heard his case. "Now I'm going to get a life," he declared, before leaving the courts in the company of Sally and his children Azariah and Jalisco.

McDowell is 'concerned' at finding

Mr McDowell: studying lengthy court judgment

By Paul Cullen

THE Minister for Justice, Mr McDowell, has expressed concern about the finding by the Court of Criminal Appeal that there was a miscarriage of justice in the case involving Frank Shortt and some Donegal gardai.

A spokesperson said Mr McDowell was "clearly concerned" about the judgment and its implications. However, he could not comment further until he had read the lengthy judgment in full.

Supt John Farrelly, of the Garda Press Office, said the force accepted the judgment handed down by the court. "We'll be studying it in full and looking at its implications," he said.

The office of the Director of Public Prosecutions, Mr James Hamilton, said he was precluded from commenting on individual cases. "We cannot confirm what may or may not happen as a result of this judgment," an official said.

Fine Gael called on Mr McDowell to outline what steps he intends to take to protect the integrity of the Garda Síochána.

The party's justice spokesman, Mr John Deasy, said the court's finding that two Garda witnesses had invented evidence was "deeply disturbing". It was essential that the entire force did not suffer as a result.

The Labour Party called for a full criminal investigation, with a file to be sent to the DPP.

Mr Joe Costello TD said the court's findings were among the most serious criticisms ever levelled against gardai by a court. "It is difficult to contemplate a more serious allegation against gardai, of up to the rank of superintendent, that they deliberately invented evidence and concealed that fact," he said. Coming on top of other recent high-profile cases, the comments of the court would only serve to undermine further public confidence in the force. Mr Costello said there was "a compelling case" for institutional reform of the Garda, including the setting up of a Garda ombudsman and an independent Garda authority.

"Everyone acknowledges that the gardai are involved in continuing battles against ruthless criminal and paramilitary gangs and in making these criticisms it is only proper to acknowledge that the vast majority of members of the force operate properly and within the law at all times.

"However, attempts at short cuts to justice are never acceptable and run the risk of a miscarriage of justice – as has happened on this occasion," said Mr Costello.

THE IRISH TIMES
travel service

ENJOY THE MAGIC OF THE WORLDS BEST FAMILY RESORT – ORLANDO

	June & September	July & August
3 Adults & 2 Children (under 12)	€6724	€7309
2 Adults & 2 Children (under 12)	€5725	€6194

(excluding taxes, insurance and car extras)

Imagine a holiday where dreams come true, fantasies become reality and unbelievable fun and relaxation all join together to provide a magical escape for your family. Whatever your idea of holiday fun, the answer can be found in the Walt Disney World Resort in Florida.

Your trip includes:
Return flights from Dublin or Shannon to Orlando – routing is via New York, Boston, Newark or London. One stopover permitted. 13 nights in a 3 bedroom villa in the Disney Area complete with TV, 2 bathrooms, fully-fitted kitchen, and private outdoor pool. Upgrade to full size 4 door car.

10-Day World Ticket to Walt Disney World Resort in Florida
Over 21 consecutive days you are entitled to 10 days' admission to all the fun of Walt Disney World Resort in Florida including: 4 Disney Theme Parks – Magic Kingdom Park, Epcot, Disney's Animal Kingdom Theme Park and Disney-MGM Studios. Great Water Parks – Disney's Blizzard Beach and Disney's Typhoon Lagoon Water Park. Downtown Disney Area – Pleasure Island, DisneyQuest Indoor Interactive Theme Park, Disney's Wide World of Sports Complex (valid only on event days, some events may require separate admission). One (1) Character Breakfast (available at participating restaurants). Complimentary use of the Walt Disney World Transportation system.

Special reduced rate on car extras at €10 per car per day
This covers local taxes, handling fees, airport fee, environmental taxes, full tank of petrol, one additional named driver, insurance excess, out of hours charges, cancellation protection, unlimited mileage, loss damage waiver and supplementary liability insurance.

All bookings are subject to the normal terms and conditions of Keith Prowse Travel – details available on request. Once confirmed, cancellation charges apply. This holiday is organised solely by Keith Prowse Travel (TA 0231) and is offered subject to availability.

Tel: 01 878 3686 quoting ITKP007
or SEND COUPON TO: THE IRISH TIMES TRAVEL SERVICE, C/O KEITH PROWSE TRAVEL, IRISH LIFE MALL, DUBLIN 1.

Mr/Mrs/Miss
Address
Tel
ITKP007
On which days do you normally buy The Irish Times?
Mon. ☐ Tues. ☐ Wed. ☐ Thurs. ☐ Fri. ☐ Sat. ☐
If you do NOT wish to receive offers from other companies carefully selected by The Irish Times, please tick this box ☐

THE IRISH TIMES
travel service

The court heard again of my time in Mountjoy. I expressed to the court how ironic it was that I was in jail for the alleged sale and supply of drugs in my premises, yet for three years I witnessed the sale, supply and possession of drugs taking place freely in Mountjoy prison every day, all day. (My expression of this thought sent some curious, startled whispers rippling throughout the courtroom.) And I told the court how during this time what kept me going was my utter belief and conviction that I would eventually have my convictions set aside and the truth would come out.

For many years after initially securing my Miscarriage of Justice Certificate in 2002, I fought tooth and claw so that I would receive the just amount of compensation not only for my own suffering but for my children's, too. They felt the wrath of this entire frenzy of injustice just as much as I did. I had a figure of damages in my head which I aimed for which I believed to be fair, I won't mention what it was - I'll just take that to the grave with me.

In October of 2005, within the Four Courts, the state awarded me a sum of 1.93 million EUR. My entire family was present and we couldn't help but feel very disappointed. I was shocked and dumbfounded. We took this as an insult from the government after everything that had happened in the case. Justice Adrian Hardiman himself had said it was 'the worst-known oppression of a citizen by the state'. Don't forget this was in the peak times of the Celtic Tiger and I knew friends who'd paid more for their houses in Dublin than the amount of compensation I was awarded and yet I had lost everything including my freedom for three years. I looked on the gesture as a quick and easy pay off which didn't have any consideration whatsoever for what my family and I had been through. I was utterly disappointed and after a short deliberation with my legal team I hastily refused and decided to fight again another day.

With the money we had received from those damages awarded in 2005, I had decided to bring my wife Sally on a trip of a lifetime round the world. I had been plagued with waiting for this entire affair to end. I initially wanted to bring Sally on this trip when I finally felt the sweet taste of success and the winds of fortune could blow us around the four corners of the world, but time was moving on so we decided to go on the trip before the next court fixture. We travelled across all continents of the globe, from South America to Asia including many Islands in the Pacific Ocean and Oceania.

I was always quite a Risk-taker, in business life and in pleasure. This was taken on our travels around the world in 2007. I believe it was a resort somewhere in the Pacific Islands.

Sally and I standing on a beach in Bora Bora, an Island in the middle of the Pacific ocean, 2007.

On board the mighty USS Arizona which was bombed at Pearl Harbour, Hawaii, in World War II

Coincidentally or maybe not, the news of my final victory over the state had come to me when I was in the most precious area of the world to both myself and Sally. It was a little seaside town called Puerto Escondido in south-west Mexico, about 200 miles south of Acapulco. It was special to us as we had lost our first son there on its beach almost 40 years before and this was my very first time re-visiting the site where we had lost our first boy. I always swore to myself and mentioned it to my family that one day I would go back but I wanted to return there a victorious man but I wasn't victorious, not until I got the phone call of the news back home. It couldn't have come at a better time or a better place than where it did. It was almost as if our deceased son Kelly had handed us the victory himself after years of failure and torment. I would have to say it was probably the proudest moment of my life. The relief of the pressure lifted from me mixed with the warm sun of Mexico beating down on my back was serene. I was, at last, the Phoenix who rose from the ashes.

Sitting on the rocks of the beach in Puerto Escondido where my first son Kelly had died. I swore that one day I would return to that beach and there I am.

Chapter Sixteen
My Vindication

Frank Shortt was the victim of "the worst-known oppression of a citizen by the state"
Mr Justice Adrian Hardiman

Ever since my release from prison 1997, I made the decree that I would rise from these ashes and achieve triumph over tyranny. Life took on a whole new meaning for me; I had a whole new game in mind. My age really had nothing to do with it; I firmly believe I would have fought this battle into my eighties if it required me to. The game was put there by me and I came, I saw, and I conquered it. I don't think the State expected it, nor do I think they expected me.

Although never really admitting that anything was wrong, the State eventually agreed to quash my conviction "for no particular stated reason".

There was large element of chance and coincidence involved in my eventual vindication. One of the Gardaí involved, Detective Noel McMahon, was a man who drank to gross excess and when drunk he confessed his perjury to two of the witnesses who gave evidence in the Court of Criminal Appeal. Secondly, McMahon's drinking problem, in the years following my case, made him into a "loose cannon" from the point of view of his fellow Gardaí and superior officers.

In evidence to the Court of Criminal Appeal, his wife Sheenagh McMahon said that her husband was "upset in front of me about Mr Shortt, and about his conviction, he didn't think that Mr Shortt was going to get three years... I don't think that he was upset about the fact he was convicted, but he was definitely upset at the fact that he was put in jail for three years... he said he didn't expect him to get three years."

Thirdly, there was something of a falling out between McMahon and Lennon over an apparently trivial cause: Lennon successfully nominated himself for a divisional policing award wholly or mainly on the basis of my conviction. Detective McMahon bitterly resented this as he felt he should have had the award himself.

Each of those men were so unscrupulous that they were quoted in the court to have "seriously frightened each other"

Kevin Lennon in the days surrounding my conviction in 1995 used to boast to his fellow Gardai 'I'll be commissioner one day"

Judge Hardiman said, and I quote, that Lennon and McMahon "seem to have borne him no personal ill-will: they did it for the purpose of furthering their own careers". Lennon got a divisional policing award. He also said that both engaged in a conspiracy to concoct false evidence against me which in turn resulted in perjured Garda evidence being given at my trial, leading to my conviction.

After receiving my Certificate of Miscarriage of Justice, Kevin Lennon received papers at his home suspending him on full pay. Garda Tina Fowley was also suspended along with Lennon. Noel McMahon was given a period of time to argue that his actions did not constitute a case for his dismissal. He was also entitled to challenge the dismissal in the courts. Shortly afterwards he resigned from the force. Lennon was later dismissed completely from the force.

We mustn't forget that these two men were involved in the framing of innocent citizens for murder, planting of explosives in order to gain promotion, unlawful arrests, mistreatment of citizens in custody, procurement of false confessions, perverting the course of justice and perjury. Although I followed the Morris Tribunal but not religiously, I don't believe either of these men or their Garda minions were ever charged in connection with any of these serious crimes and I don't believe they ever will.

Chief Justice Mr Justice John Murray said that I had been the victim of disreputable conduct and a shocking abuse of power on the part of those two Garda officers.

The judgment showed that I was an innocent man and finally my name was now vindicated and cleared.

On 17 May, 2006, the second and final day of the hearing of my appeal, leading counsel for the defendants Mr Michael Cush SC resumed his submissions with the announcement that he would be saying, as he aptly put it, "something by way of apology to Mr Shortt". At the conclusion of his submissions he said that he wished to:

"... take the opportunity to say that the state acknowledges that Mr Frank Shortt was the victim of a grave miscarriage of justice. For that and for all his suffering and loss in consequence the state apologises to him unreservedly."

This apology was given to me 14 years after the start of the chain of events which led to my wrongful conviction of drug offences on the basis of consciously false Garda evidence, 11 years after I was sentenced, five-and-a-half years after my conviction was quashed by the consent of the Director of Public Prosecutions, and just under four years after the declaration by the Court of Criminal Appeal that my conviction was a miscarriage of justice.

I just felt from the pit of my stomach that the apology was both belated and limited in the sense that no apology of any kind was offered until the Court was surprised to hear the previous day that in fact an apology was absent. The apology was carefully drafted, it did not refer to my innocence, and there was no inkling that it was offered on behalf of An Garda Síochána either. I accepted it in the spirit in which it was offered.

ABUSE OF POWER

MIRROR, Saturday, August 3, 2002

SHAME OF POWER

Bent Garda Lennon:

EXCLUSIVE

By DECLAN FAHY

CROOKED Garda Superintendent Kevin Lennon is today exposed as a power freak who was determined to get to the top at any cost.

The senior officer, who helped put innocent nightclub owner Frank Shortt behind bars on false drugs charges, used to boast: "I'll be Commissioner one day".

Sources told the Irish Daily Mirror that Lennon had a loyal team of five officers who would do whatever he ordered in North Donegal.

The activities of these officers have now resulted in a string of lawsuits from innocent people that could cost the state millions.

Two of Lennon's team have been suspended and two are under investigation. Proceedings are being prepared against another.

Mr Shortt's appeal court hearing was told that Lennon and his friend Detective Noel McMahon had planted explosives in North Donegal – then Lennon sent out Gardaí to find them.

It was alleged the two corrupt officers did it to boost their prospects for promotion. They deny this.

But now the state is facing huge payouts after the homes of innocent people were raided for Provo bombs.

A woman, a school principal and her landowner husband were shocked when their property was searched by detectives.

The source said: "Their names were blackened because of what happened – even though they were as pure as the driven snow.

"They have launched legal action and are set to win

SHAMED: Det Noel McMahon, above, and Supt Kevin Lennon

'Lennon thought he was king of Donegal'

damages in the court. But they are not the only ones. Several other decent, law-abiding people who had their homes raided are also taking action.

"The public just know about the Shortt and McBrearty cases. But there is a whole can of worms to come out.

"When these other cases come to court, the Gardaí in Donegal are not going to look good at all."

The Irish Daily Mirror can reveal that no-one else was ever charged following several raids that resulted in Lennon's finds.

These are separate claims to those being made by Frank Shortt and publican Frank McBrearty, who say they were harassed by Gardaí for years.

A source added: "Lennon thought he was king of Donegal. He was a Superintendent in a powerful position, and no-one would dare question his orders.

"When he arrived in Buncrana, several officers were shocked at his behaviour – but could do nothing.

"It was as if the whole area was his own personal fiefdom. He was power hungry from his early days."

Lennon, a native of Co Leitrim, comes from a long line of Gardaí – several of his brothers are in the force.

The source added: "When Lennon was a Garda in Buncrana he would stick his chest out and tell colleagues that he was going to be Commissioner.

"He got a post as a Superintendent's clerk in the station, where he knew everything that was going on.

"After that, he was transferred to Letterkenny on promotion to Sergeant."

He was later promoted to Inspector in Buncrana, a rank he held at the time of the raid on Frank Shortt's night club in 1992.

The source added: "Then he became Superintendent. By now he was in control of a huge area.

"He had his own team. All the time he had his eye on greater things.

"But all the explosives finds were starting to raise

AN OFFICER FREAK

I'll be Commissioner one day

Where's my APOLOGY? asks Frank

FRANK Shortt yesterday said he was disappointed the Garda Commissioner and the Justice Minister had not yet offered an apology to him or his family.

He said: "What my wife Sally, myself and the rest of my family are a little bit disturbed about is that the Minister for Justice and the Garda Commissioner have not bothered to telephone me or my wife and say, 'we apologise, we're sorry'."

Mr Shortt maintains senior people outside the Garda Siochana were involved in the conspiracy that led to his wrongful conviction for allowing drugs to be sold in his club.

The Court of Appeal ruled on Thursday that the conviction was a miscarriage of justice.

Mr Shortt told Donegal's Highland Radio yesterday: "Nothing will compensate me for the years in jail.

"But I don't feel any animosity towards those two men, Kevin Lennon and Noel McMahon.

"After all, they have wives and they have children and it would be very, very wrong to condemn them.

"They are human beings like you and me and I believe their families are suffering."

INNOCENT MAN: Nightclub boss Frank Shortt

eyebrows. More senior officers were wondering how come so many finds were being made.

"Lennon believed he was on the fast track to the top.

"Then the McBrearty thing blew up. The McBrearty family told how they had been harassed for years by Gardaí."

An Assistant Commissioner, Kevin Carty, was sent to Donegal to look into the affair. McMahon was suspended and Lennon was transferred from the area and put behind a desk at Garda headquarters in Dublin.

Frank Shortt had been jailed in 1995 for three years on evidence deliberately invented by McMahon and Lennon.

The Court of Criminal Appeal set aside his conviction in 2000.

On Wednesday his jailing was deemed to be a miscarriage of justice. Lennon was suspended in disgrace on Thursday night.

The targeting of Frank Shortt and Frank McBrearty

HOUNDED: Frank McBrearty

also lost the Gardaí close friends. A source said: "Both men had always co-operated with the force.

"McBrearty couldn't do enough for Gardaí before he was targeted in the wrong over the death of cattle dealer Richie Barron.

"Frank Shortt too was a respected member of the community who was helpful to the force."

Lennon's actions also interfered with Special Branch operations against the IRA in Donegal.

A source said: "People were being harassed by Gardaí - yet many of these people were secretly helping Special Branch in the war against the IRA."

● LAST night, Frank Shortt backed the Irish Mirror's revelations that up to six members of the Gardaí were involved in his wrongful conviction.

He said: "It is not just two members of the Gardaí. I understand there are five or six involved.

"I do believe it is bigger than that. How big I don't know. I think we are talking about others outside the Gardaí."

The barrister acting for the prosecution pointed out the evidence against me was very weak. Whereas there was evidence that drugs had been sold on the premises, there was no evidence that I ever knew about it.

My punitive damages portion was increased from €50,000 to €1m. This is thought to be the largest ever punitive damages award in the history of the State. I remember when I first saw the figures, I smiled, not at the amount so to speak, but to the difference between the two figures.

The increase of punitive damages to 1 million euro was to reflect the court's disapproval of what Chief Justice John Murray described as an affair which was "a stain of the darkest dye on the otherwise generally fine tradition of the Garda" and the "especially grave abuse of Mr Shortt by two Gardai-Supterintendent Kevin Lennon and Detective Garda Noel McMahon". According to Mr Justice Murray, I had been the victim of "dis-reputable conduct and a shocking abuse of power". He concluded by saying my experience was "a tormenting saga of imprisonment, mental and physical deterioration, estrangement from family, loss of business, public and professional ignominy and despair". He was sacrificed in order to assist the career ambitions of a number of members of the Garda".

The total damages were increased from 1.93 million in October 2005 to 4.6 million in 2007. Although I never will discuss with anyone outside my family the actual figure I was aiming for, let's just say that I was happy with the final settlement.

I remember saying to the press, something which they later quoted in the newspapers ' This is probably going to sound strange, but I wouldn't want anyone to end up in prison like I did. Prison is a terrible place and these people have families to think about. I suppose that's just the kind of person I am.'

In the end I didn't mind at all coming across as having no grudges or thoughts about seeking revenge for those who harmed me and my family. I felt it more important to show the public and the state that hate shouldn't always breed hate.

Shortly after my total vindication I received very humble apologies from both the Taoiseach Bertie Ahern and the President Mary McAleese. Bertie's apology came in the form of a very nice letter which I keep among my files to this day. Mary's apology came in the form of a phone call she made to me personally. We had a lengthy conversation, a lot of which didn't involve the case but more trivial matters. Mrs McAleese then very kindly invited Sally and I to have dinner together with her and her husband in Áras an Uachtaráin. We never did get around to having that dinner in the Presidential residence for whatever reason, and Mrs McAleese is no longer the president, but the telephone conversation we had will suffice as an apology from the state and will forever stand in my memory.

I often wondered would I receive a formal apology from the Garda Commissioner on behalf of An Garda Siochana. It never came.

I don't believe either of the two officers or indeed any Gardai were punished for their treachery and unlawful behaviour in Donegal in the nineties. At this stage I don't believe they ever will.

HomeNews

Court rejects garda's health objection to tribunal

Chief Justice says affair was "a stain of the darkest dye" on tradition of the Garda Síochána

Supreme Court increases Shortt awards to €4.7m

MARY CAROLAN

Hardiman says innocent man 'perjured into prison'

MARY CAROLAN

Case highlights need for reform - Minister

CONOR LALLY, CRIME CORRESPONDENT

Prison criticised over methadone delay

One of the many articles which spanned the country and the globe upon my final vindication in 2007

Chapter Seventeen
THE CHILDREN

What hurt me the most in this entire crisis was the effect that the situation had on my children. I felt helpless when they needed me and I couldn't be there for them. I'm sure any parent would feel the same in such a predicament.

I knew through my wife Sally that our children had become very traumatised and difficult since I was snatched from them. They were subject to endless taunts and remarks, not just at school but whenever they went out in public.

They had always applied for summer jobs, but now if they stated their names and who they were, there were no jobs available for them. My wife was having a desperate time trying to keep things going. We were in ruins after the Point Inn was burned to the ground.

Each and every one of our children was terribly affected.

Jalisco, who had helped me so much in the running of the Point Inn, had lost all interest after it burnt down. He tried to get other jobs but nobody would hire him because he was a Shortt. He was reduced to spending days slumped in front of the television, in a state of total depression. Eventually he got a job as a part-time barman in Moville, but had to give it up because so many of the customers taunted him. After my release, I worked to get him motivated. He went on to gain a degree in satellite communications, but still had problems getting employment, thanks to his family name.

*My Son Jalisco with my grandson Reece
on Jalisco's wedding day in June 2007*

Natasha had also worked at the Point Inn, in the bar. After my imprisonment she tried to get a job locally but like Jalisco she was turned down again and again. Eventually, she opted to leave the country altogether and emigrated to Germany where she lived for many years. She currently lives in Sicily with her husband and 4 children, a place where she is not known or judged by her surname, a place where she is happy and away from it all.

My Daughter Natasha standing on Stroove Beach near Greencastle, Co.Donegal. In her arms is her son and my grandson Kristian. He was named after my son Kristian around the time of Kristian's stabbing.

My middle daughter Zabrina was in the community school in Carndonagh and went through a pretty rotten time once the word got about her father's "drug offences" and jail sentence. She did not say very much because she is a quiet person, but I knew that deep down she was very hurt. In a strong kind of manner she was able to block out all the torment and abuse which was thrown at her from the mouths of her peers. I think that her only way of dealing with the situation, in her belief, was to just lower her head, take it all on the chin and hope to grow up fast. Despite all the harassment she grew to be a fine woman and lives in Dublin today and runs her own business.

My Daughter Zabrina

My youngest daughter, Azariah, was only twelve years old when I was imprisoned. She also attended the community school. On one occasion, the religion teacher talked about what happened to people who broke the law – they finished up in a place called Mountjoy. As he was making these remarks, he was looking directly at Azariah. She came home in tears. Azariah suffered many taunts from her fellow classmates in School and to this day would seldom talk about it because it pains her too much. I remember Azariah once telling of how one particular girl attacked her and hurting her badly. When I asked Azariah why this girl attacked her, she told me that this girl became very aggressive the moment Azariah became defensive of her father. I remember when I was growing up, girls tended to be of a more refined type, not this girl. I would easily believe that some senior member of her family wanted or maybe even instructed her to attack my daughter.

My Daughter Azariah with her son and my grandson Reuben.

And then there is my youngest son, Kristian.

When I think on the life my youngest son has lived since 1994 I become exhausted. Although all our children were hurt, from the very beginning of my imprisonment back in 1994, through all that ensued right up to the present day, the abuse that my youngest son Kristian has suffered has been dreadful and never ending. He also attended Carndonagh Community School, and was subjected to endless taunting and attacks by bullies. One of these two bullies broke his nose and called his father a "drug-dealing scumbag". Due to the fierce bullying we had to remove Kristian from Carndonagh Community School and place him in a Boarding School in Co. Tipperary called Rockwell College.

Kristian suffered many numerous assaults in Donegal throughout his twenties but on the 8th October 2008, whilst attending a party in an apartment on Main Street in Letterkenny, Kristian was stabbed seventeen times by a man in a frenzied attack. He suffered stab wounds to the neck, head, back and chest. His jugular vein was slashed, and one thrust just missed his heart. The man also slit Kristian's throat. It was an unbelievably savage attack.

As soon as I heard about the attack I rushed to Letterkenny General Hospital. Kristian was still alive – he is very strong and a fighter. He fought tooth and nail for his life. When his condition began to worsen he was then transferred to St Vincent's Hospital in Dublin for emergency surgery. We lost him twice on the operating table – once for as long as thirty seconds. It seemed all over for him.

After surgery, he remained in critical condition. His chances for survival were minimal. We held a vigil at his bedside. Yet my son was so brave in the heart that he managed to pull through against all odds, shocking not only us but his doctors and surgeons.

Kristian's attacker is a member of a notorious Dublin gang, who at this point I'm not at liberty to name. He was apprehended at a Garda checkpoint on the Tyrone-Monaghan border. He was questioned and charged with the assault and the book of evidence was later served on him in Letterkenny Court around November 2008. Yet this man has not stood trial for the attempted murder of my son almost four years ago. He is free to walk the streets of Dublin. My son Kristian informs me that there were "glitches" with his arrest and charging and so neither the judicial system nor the Gardaí have managed to bring him to court.

Kristian suffered another attempt on his life in 2010. This time a group of men were waiting for him outside the Voodoo Bar in Letterkenny.

It was the night of 26th July and Kristian was leaving the bar around one in the morning, accompanied by his sister Zabrina and his girlfriend, Louise. As he was crossing the street with the girls to get into a taxi, he received a terrible blow to the back of his head. His attacker used a knuckleduster against Kristian's skull. My son dropped to his knees in the middle of the street. Another one of the men – a martial arts specialist – then kicked the kneeling Kristian in the face, sending him flying backwards. His head hit the ground and split open. He was bleeding from his eyes and ears. Then all of the men attempted to kick my unconscious son to death. The girls threw themselves down across his body, Zabrina protecting his head and Louise his chest, determined to save his life. The men ordered the girls to get out of the way; they tried to physically pull them off Kristian's body. They shouted: "We're going to kill him!" The girls were screaming, holding on to my son's body with all their strength. I saw their clothes the following day, covered with his blood.

The security men from the Voodoo Bar ran over and warned the men away from Kristian's body, but they wouldn't leave.

An ambulance arrived and the entire street was blocked off. Kristian spent the night in Letterkenny General Hospital. He regained consciousness the following day.

Even though the whole attack was captured by CCTV, no-one to this day has been arrested for the attack.

The final straw came for Kristian came on the 8th January 2011. He had not socialised in Letterkenny since the night of his savage attack six months previously, but that night he decided to return to the Voodoo Bar with his girlfriend.

Shortly afterwards a man approached Kristian with two other men. The man told Kristian that they were going to kill him that night and if they didn't kill him in the pub then they would come to his house afterwards to finish the job. The man's friends took up positions at the exits. One pulled a knife out of his pocket and showed it to Kristian. Kristian moved himself and his girlfriend underneath a CCTV camera and began pointing up to it, hoping that it would act as a deterrent for the men not to approach. Meanwhile, his girlfriend called the Gardaí.

The Gardaí told Kristian's girlfriend that they couldn't come into the bar and insisted she bring Kristian outside. She told the Gardaí that the men had pulled a knife and had blocked off the exits. The Gardaí still refused to come into the premises. It was getting on for closing time. Kristian called one of the detectives in charge of his previous stabbing case and told him: "If you don't come down to Voodoo to escort me the hell out of these premises then it's very possible that I will be leaving these premises in a f..king body bag and my blood will be on your hands and the hands of the Gardaí."

The detective arrived down immediately with some fellow Gardaí, came into the bar and escorted Kristian from the premises. The men followed them out of the pub and stood openly waiting for the Gardai to drive off, leaving Kristian unprotected. The detective waited with Kristian and his girlfriend until a taxi came and took them home. As the men had threatened to follow him home, Kristian took the taxi to my house in Moville, forty five minutes away.

Who was the man who issued the death threats against Kristian in the Voodoo that night?

He was the son of one of the Gardai involved in the campaign against The Point Inn and the Shortt family.

Are these attacks somehow linked to the case against me? Perhaps we will never know.

After that final incident, Kristian decided that enough was enough and left the Donegal area completely.

My son Kristian enjoying a Guinness in Jacksons Hotel, Ballybofey, Co.Donegal in 2012

Chapter Eighteen
HORIZONS REACHED

Out of suffering have emerged the strongest souls; the most massive characters are seared with scars.
Kahlil Gibran

My twilight years have advanced all around me now. I'm an old man with a young German Shepherd to keep me company on my long walks down by the shore or in the countryside surrounding my house. I once had an abundance of energy and spirit but the last twenty years of my life has taken its toll. I am covered with emotional scars from head to foot – but my journeys are made more interesting by my far-ranging thoughts. There are many little stories which I will bring to the grave with me but I definitely feel that my story of persecution and injustice is one that I've always wanted to share with my family, my friends and many more. In the end I hope I've done myself justice and made my family proud of me.

Holding my grandchild Zara in 2006 , daughter of my son Jalisco.

If I'm not walking the countryside then I'm enjoying a glass of red wine out in my conservatory along with my wife Sally, and occasionally with my five children and many grandchildren. My youngest son Kristian will soon be bringing me another grandchild so life in many ways is still fulfilling. I embrace each sunset as if it were my last and I'm exceedingly happy to be alive and experiencing a full life.

Outside my house in the winter of 2008, heading off on a Winters day walk.

There were times in Mountjoy Prison when I would honestly say I didn't think I was going to make it out with my life. I don't in any way feel grudges toward any of the people who wronged me, not just over the past twenty years but throughout my entire life. I feel that if I carried bitterness along with me in my journey through life, I would walk into my horizon with a heavy heart.

Now I sit in my conservatory with the sun touching my face and I find myself smiling for no apparent reason. I reminisce about my life, not only the injustice but my life in its entirety, right back to my playful days as a boy in Ballyshannon in West Donegal.

I think back to when I lost my first little boy in Puerto Escondido, on the south-west coast of Mexico.

While Sally and I were living in Canada, we decided to go on the trip of a lifetime. We got ourselves a camper van and headed for Mexico with the intention of driving all the way around South America and back again.

Sitting with my son Kelly enjoying the sun in Mexico. In the background is an Aztec Temple, 1971.

Reaching the beautiful beach at Puerto Escondido, on the south-west coast of Mexico, I remember sitting back in the hot sun with two ex-Marine friends of mine, Arthur and Greg. Then I noticed that my son Kelly, whom I used to call Bodelle, had vanished from our company. Myself and the two marines became slightly worried – where had he gone? We began to search for him, along with my wife Sally. When ten minutes grew into twenty minutes we grew edgy, and every minute thereafter felt like an eternity as we searched the entire beach and surrounding area.

Suddenly, out of the corner of my eye, I saw Arthur running along the beach towards us with Kelly in his arms. Kelly's head was arched back and he wasn't moving. Arthur had found him lying face down in a small rock pool on the fringe of the beach.

The only thought that ran through my head was: "Please God, please God, let him be okay". We ran at a frantic pace towards Arthur. When we reached him we could see that Kelly lay lifeless in his arms. Sally took him from Arthur's arms and put him down on the wet hard sand. Sally was a nurse so immediately she began to give our little boy CPR to save his life. I stood watching from above. It was as if I were struck by a lightning bolt. I couldn't move or think as shock and confusion began to bombard my mind.

I looked down as Sally performed the CPR while thumping Kelly's chest in a desperate attempt to revive his heart. After minutes there was still no response and Sally became hectic and petrified. I dropped to my knees as I didn't have the strength any more to stand and watch my boy dying in front of my eyes. I knelt down on my knees looking at his beautiful face and his long blond hair, wishing he would just draw a breath. I looked to the sky and pleaded with God not to take my boy. Sally began crying in complete horror.

Our little boy Kelly had gone. We'd lost him.

She never gave up though – she kept beating on his chest and performing CPR for another forty five minutes until I had to take her away. She would have been there until the sun set trying to bring her first little boy back to this world. I could do nothing but carry his lifeless body with his long blonde hair wrapped around my arm. I put his body in the camper van.

My wife Sally and son Kelly feeding the birds along one of the great northern lakes in Canada, 1969.

My wife Sally and Son Kelly bathing together on a beach somewhere in Canada, 1969.

We drove all the way back to Mexico City with the body of Kelly behind us in the camper van. We put him on ice to preserve his body until we got there, where we had his body cremated. He was almost three years old.

All the words in the world can't describe our devastation. All the most beautiful words in the world can't describe how much of an angel our little boy was. Such are the harsh lessons of life: no matter how good something is, it must come to an end – sometimes sooner, sometimes later. It was the time we spent with Kelly that we learned to fully appreciate and we simply couldn't dread our creator for such a tragedy.

We returned to Ireland with Kelly's ashes. He now lies in an urn in our bedroom, sometimes on top of the locker, sometimes by the window. And every spring without fail we place a vase with daffodils on top of his urn by the window. He greets me when I wake up in the morning and when I go to bed at night. His memory lingers in my mind while his body is perched on our window.

As I mentioned before there are many things I will bring to the grave with me and, originally, the following story was one of them. But perhaps maybe I could instil some hope for some with this story. One night as I lay in bed beside Sally the most peculiar thing occurred. I was fast asleep and usually I would sleep even through a storm. All of a sudden I felt something brush off my feet at the bottom of the bed. Before I even raised my head to look down to the bottom of the bed I had a feeling in my bones that something was there waiting to grasp my attention. The hairs on my arms stood up even before I dared to look.

I took a breath and raised my head to look. Before my eyes could reach the bottom of the bed they were met by a glow. Then I rested my eyes on the vision, and the vision was Kelly. He sat at the bottom of the bed by my feet with a mysterious blue glow oozing out from his body. His skin looked very vibrant. He just sat there and smiled at me. I turned to wake up Sally but when we both looked back to the bottom of the bed, he was gone. I often wonder why he didn't remain there for Sally to see him also.

I don't think a day goes by when I don't think upon that fateful day and how it changed Sally's and my life. There will always be that sense of loss in our hearts for our little boy. My only consolation is my belief that one day soon I will be reunited with him again. I've missed him so much that I suppose there isn't too much of a sadness when I think of my death. Perhaps that is the Almighty's plan, perhaps that is God's design, to make death not such an insufferable burden for me to endure, for I will be greeted by my little boy at the pearly gates.

Will he be a boy as I remember him, the same boy that appeared to my youngest son Kristian in the hour of his death when my little boy sat like the Buddha, smiling at Kristian and guarding his life? Or will he be a grown man with whom I can share my stories, along long walks in Paradise? It's a mystery, one of the many mysteries that have made my life worth living and possibly even worth a glimpse – but that's not for the faint-hearted. It's certainly been a journey of discovery with some horrible moments, yet some moments worthy of the Gods themselves.

My brothers and I fishing on lough Erne, Co. Fermanagh. My brother Jim is on my right and Louis to my left holding a massive Pike fish, Bernard Jnr is on the far right.

Epilogue

And so I leave you now with a letter which I wrote to my living brothers and sisters when I was sentenced to prison in 1995. I bid you farewell and adieu.

A Farewell From A Prisoner To His Sisters And Brothers

Teresa, Cecelia, Joe and Mick

Lord of the far horizons,
Give us the eyes to see
Over the verge of the Sunset
The Beauty that is to be.
Bliss Carman

He was beginning to taste the joy of loneliness. No room for vanities in his wilderness. He yielded to nothing a thousand times and the pain of suffering was more enlightening than the allure of surrender, for a voice from within, whispering and echoing back over three generations, had urged him onwards, reminding him of the hardships which the decent old people had endured with a Tear and a Smile. The principles they stood for and their memories had to be honoured and their own struggle had to be acknowledged and respected. There could be no yielding now, there could never have been, no expediency for the benefit of short term gain, no capitulation to the surrogates of cheap evil games played by knaves. His Rubicon had been crossed and he detested failure. He had realised that the moment of truth has almost arrived where his every decision and reaction will be viewed by his family with concern for their futures, for he must now become the embodiment of principle and unshakeable determination, a man with a cause and a sense of his own value and what that means to his wife and their children. The price paid was far too great to be squandered or frittered away at the last moment in exchange for freedom so that those profane witnesses who insulted their oaths to Almighty God might be shielded and remain incognito. No, there could not be any yielding to the likes of such people who inhumanly and unjustly committed him to the solitude of a prison cell, too cold in winter and too hot in summer, the sleepless nights and nightmares. The die is cast, the scene is set, and now let come what may, the moment of truth is rapidly closing and this prisoner will not be found wanting for Truth is by his side. The enemy must now smart under his Lash.

What this prisoner has done and the stand he has taken will be remembered in his family for generations and it must be remembered with pride, not with indignation. The next generation expect that a torch will be passed on so as to inspire and guide them in the way of righteousness in case a similar injustice be inflicted upon one of them.

In this, sometimes profane world, the hollow sounding voice of perjurers, begrudgers and defamers must be silenced. Their sole reward must only be that adjudged appropriate by the Supreme Arbiter from whose perfect judgement there shall be no appeal. And in the mid-twenty first century when our young ancestors, blood of our blood, meet and relate the story of their grandfather who has been unjustly imprisoned in Mountjoy Gulag they will not need to lie when they proudly boast "he had courage to resist the might of Big Brother and he was right".

So farewell to the last of his heroes who stood firm and faithful to the end. What new trials or ordeals will be placed in their paths in seasons to come to test their patience, endurance and character when this brother has found peace and freedom at last. To every back the burden and what further sorrows shall be placed their way before that Great Power which controls all shall say: "Enough, come enter the Kingdom where I have a very special place prepared for you". For what are trials, sorrows and tribulations but stepping stones to guide you to Paradise.

"All my trials Lord soon be over."
Goodbye Noble Champions.
Frank Bosco
Mountjoy Gulag

Many of the Shortt gang posing for a photo outside The Point Inn in 1972. From left to right...Mick, Cecelia, Jim, Peggy, My mother Cecelia and Father Bernard, Fr Raphael, Teresa, Joe, Louis and Myself', the children in the picture are Mike, Bernard, Ethna, Fiona, Jim, Aidan, Gerard, Bernadette and Paula.

Appendix One

LETTER TO MINISTER OF JUSTICE MR. PADRAIG FLYNN

THE POINT INN

QUIGLEY'S POINT, CO. DONEGAL   Telephone: Quigley's Point (x) 077-83021

ENTERTAINMENT CENTRE OF THE NORTH-WEST

Contact : F. B. Shortt
Home Tel. 077-82400

Mr. Padraig Flynn, T.D.
Minister for Justice
Dail Eireann
Dublin

05 August 1992

Dear Minister,

Last Sunday night our premises were subjected to a raid by sixty or so Gardai dressed in riot gear. A Search Warrant was not served on me prior to the enforced entry and invasion of my property by the Gardai though an effort was made at a later stage in the night to do so by the Garda Inspector in charge of the raid.

I did not in any way impede or attempt to interfere with the Gardai personnel though the first wave of riot police assaulted me at the main entrance to our Restaurant. When I did attempt to enquire from some Gardai as to what was going on I was told " Fuck off and mind your own business " and here I do apologize for repeating that vulgarity in my letter. As far as the three hundred or so customers on our premises at the time were concerned I witnessed no display of resistance or aggression towards the Gardai with one exception ; a girl hurled quite considerable verbal abuse at some members of the Force because her boyfriend was arrested and dragged from the premises. This lady was also arrested. Many boys and girls were abused and manhandled and also handcuffed and as for their civil liberties and rights, these were disgracefully ignored by the Gardai.

I have prepared a memo of incidents witnessed by my wife and I and also by some of our children who were on duty in our night club.

Frankly Sir, I find the entire incident to be disgraceful and in my books a case of classical "overkill". The attitude and behaviour of that riot squad does little, in my opinion, for the credibility, good name and most of all Goodwill of the Garda Siochana. As for the apparent cause which triggered such

Letter to Padraig Flynn

This was a sign above the main entrance to the nightclub.

ABUSE OF POWER

August 19

Attention all Security Staff

1. Illegal Drugs

Some degree of attention is being focused on The Point Inn by those engaged in the illegal drugs business. Attempts are being made by "drug pushers" to use our customers in an effort to boost their earnings from the sale of such drugs. It is of the utmost importance to the good name of our business that this form of activity does not succeed. Maximum attention must, therefore, be concentrated on everyone entering our premises at the beginning of the night and anyone even remotely suspect must be searched. Those who refuse to be searched cannot gain admission.

During the course of the night all security staff must continually circulate throughout the building paying close attention to groups of people assembling in corners or in toilets. Bar staff have been alerted to this drugs threat and will assist you in surveillance.

Surveillance of our car parks must also be continuous during the night and particular attention paid to anyone paying frequent visits to the fresh air.

2. In case of Emergency

(a) Head of our security will inform you of your duties in the event of an emergency.

(b) Every man must know the location of our fire exits and also our fire extinguishers.

(c) If a fire should occur it must be attacked immediately, no matter how small, with fire extinguishers.
Fires must never be given a chance.

(d) In case of a bomb alert every door in the entire building must first be opened before customers are asked to leave. Customers must then be asked to remain calm, not to run but to walk quickly through the nearest exit.

(e) All staff are expected to remain at their post and to carry out their duties during all emergencies.

3. Remember, our customers pay our wages. Please be helpful and courteous at all times.

Staff notices to be adhered to within The Point Inn.

Appendix Two
EVIDENCE OF SUPERINTENDENT BRIAN N. KENNY

Superintendent Kenny examined by Mr. Mills, Senior Counsel for the D.P.P.

Q8: Did you ever have conversations with Mr. Shortt about the matters the jury is dealing with today, matters about drugs, shall we say?
A: *I had a conversation; I had several meetings with Mr. Shortt. I had a conversation, the last one being... which was also a meeting on his premises on the 9th June, 1992.*

(Superintendent Kenny had only two meetings with me. This was to be the beginning of his tenuous evidence to the Court.)

Q11: How many earlier ones did you have?
A: *I had a meeting with him and his wife, Sally, in my office in Buncrana on the 21st April, 1992.*

Q14: Now, we will take it in sequence – the meeting of the 21st April, was that invited by you.
A: *The meeting on the 21st April was as a result of correspondence and phone calls made to me by Mr. Shortt requesting for me to meet him, on the 21st April. Mr. Shortt and his wife, Sally, arrived in my office at Buncrana Garda Station.*

(The superintendent's answer is once again not correct. There had been no correspondence prior to our meeting on 21st April 1992. I telephoned the Superintendent on Monday, 20th April. There was just one phone call and I did not write to the Superintendent before the 17th May 1992, the date of my first letter to him.)

Q16: He was complaining about the Garda inspections under the licensing laws?
A: *That's correct, my lord, yes. Between the 21ˢᵗ April and the 9ᵗʰ June correspondence passed between Mr. Shortt and myself.*

(It is important to note that the Superintendent's previous reference to the 9ᵗʰ June was in regard to a meeting. In his above answer to Q16 he now refers to correspondence on the 9ᵗʰ June. However, a short time later, when being cross-examined by my Senior Counsel he denied that he had received correspondence from me on the 8th June. You will recall from an earlier chapter, that I faxed a letter to the Superintendent on the 8ᵗʰ June and that fax was subsequently "discovered" in his Garda File. That is obviously the correspondence which the Superintendent referred to above in answer to Q16).

Q18: Do you have copies of the letters you wrote?
A: *Those letters were handed in as exhibits at the hearing in Letterkenny Court at the request of the Defence.*

(The superintendent's answer would seem to indicate that those exhibits were not in court, or is that a reasonable assumption? Perhaps they were or ought to have been. Those exhibits would have revealed my fax of the 9ᵗʰ June 1992. Who is culpable for not having those important exhibits in court? If they had been in court and were presented to the judge the trial might very well have come to an abrupt end, so important was that correspondence.)

Q24: Well, anyway, you met on the 9ᵗʰ June?
A: *I met Mr. Shortt and his wife, Sally, in his room on the 9ᵗʰ June.*

Q27: Well, here, again – what matters were debated between you?
A: *I discussed with Mr. Shortt the points raised in relation to the inspections under the Liquor Licensing Laws which were carried out by the Gardaí and in some cases Prosecutions resulted. I also gave him a reply to the allegations that he had made, that crimes concerning his property were not properly investigated.*

(The prosecutions he refers to were not instigated until after I lodged a serious complaint with the Garda Siochana Complaints Board following the major Garda assault on my business in August 1992. These prosecutions were in respect of petty violations of the Intoxicating Liquor Acts but most of all they were meant to justify, for the benefit of the Garda Complaints Board and the Garda Commissioner, the unprecedented harassment of our business by the local sergeant long before there were any illegal drugs in our area.)

Q30: Did you make any reference to the ongoing disco that he appeared to be having at the time?
A: *At the latter part of our meeting I mentioned both to Mr. and Mrs. Shortt that they were running a rave disco on their premises, which I was of the opinion was drug-related.*

(The previous day, the 8th June, Sergeant John McPhillips accompanied by seven other Gardaí carried out two thorough searches of our nightclub. The first search was carried out while our patrons were present and the second was carried out immediately after everyone had left the dance. That sergeant was later to testify that neither he nor his men had found any illegal drugs nor had they noticed any traces of illegal substances. So, where was the justification for the superintendent's opinion that our disco was drug related? Was he guessing?)

Q31: Did he respond to that?
A: *He said that the dances were not, and then stated that if they were, how could he prevent it, or something to that - I am not exactly sure what he said. I clearly remember telling Mr. Shortt that the obvious way to prevent any such alleged drug dealing - any such alleged drugs at a dance would be to cease running such type of dance. He replied, "No way". He did suggest that he would put up notices.*

(I ask the reader to please focus on part of the witness's response to the Prosecutor, his counsel, "I am not exactly sure what he said." Compare this carefully with the answer which the Superintendent was to give later on to my defence counsel when it was suggested to him that Frank Shortt would give evidence to state that the superintendent had never made such a suggestion at that meeting. The superintendent's response then would be: "My lord, I have a clear recollection of what Mr. Shortt said on that day."

Can the evidence of this witness be relied upon? This goes to the very root of my defence. At one point in his evidence the witness tells the court that he is not exactly sure what was said by me at our meeting of the 9th June 1992 and almost in the next breath he tells the Court that he has a clear recollection of what I had said.)

Q32: Like what?
A: *He suggested putting up a notice, "no drugs here" or "no drugs allowed", something in that respect. I advised him not to take such a course, as, in my view, it would only encourage people dabbling in drugs to come to his premises.*

(Both my wife and I are absolutely certain that Superintendent Kenny did not tell me to cease running our dances. If a Superintendent of the Garda Siochana tells you to cease running something it is highly unlikely that such a demand would not be heeded let alone forgotten. Why should he issue such a demand? He had no grounds for doing so. The warnings on the posters which I proposed placing on the walls around our dance hall were much stronger than what the superintendent told the Court. Many of the posters would carry words to the effect that 'pushers' would be handed over to the Gardaí. Appendix 1 displays a photograph of a poster measuring 10Ft by 3Ft. which was hung over our reception desk immediately following the Garda raid on our nightclub on 3rd August 1992. Following that raid, less than two months after our meeting with Superintendent Kenny, I placed many such posters around the inside walls of our nightclub. I cannot comprehend the Superintendent's view that such notices would attract people dabbling in drugs to come to our nightclub. Surely the contrary would be the case.)

Q36: Well, were you aware of the steps he (Inspector Kevin Lennon) was taking in the course of your continued presence in Donegal?
A: *I was aware of the steps that Inspector Lennon was carrying out. On occasions he would brief me, but having said that, I was satisfied that he would carry out my instructions thoroughly.*

Witness cross-examined by Mr. Barry White, S.C. for the Defence

Q39: The first meeting was a meeting that took place you say on the 21st April 1992?
A: *That was in my office in Buncrana, yes.*

Q41: That meeting had been prompted by correspondence that had passed between yourself and Mr. Shortt?
A: *That is correct, my lord.*

(Once again Superintendent Kenny misleads the court. Refer back to his response to Q14.)

Q52: Didn't he point out to you that his brother had died approximately a year before this meeting?
A: *He mentioned about his brother all right, but I wasn't too long stationed in Buncrana then, and I wasn't aware of Mr. Shortt prior to his meeting on the 21st.*

(In response to Q14 and 041 Superintendent Kenny told the court that the meeting had come about "as a result of correspondence and phone calls made to me by Mr. Shortt". Now he says that he was not aware of me prior to our meeting of 21st April 1992.)

Q54: And didn't he tell you that the premises had only been opened a very short time at that stage?
A: *It would have been opened a short time, that's correct, yes.*

Q55: How long do you recall had it in fact been open?
A: *From memory, it could have been two/three weeks/a month.*

Q56: Was it not much more recent than two or three weeks or a month – wasn't it only opened approximately a week?
A: *If Mr. Shortt says so I would have to accept that, as I said, I have no - it was either a week, two weeks, or a month, I am not particularly...*

Q57: Wasn't the 21st April, 1992 a Tuesday?
A: *It would have been, yes, as far as I can recollect.*

Q58: And hadn't the licensed premises only been re-opened at the weekend prior to that?
A: *I am not particularly sure on that, my lord.*

Q59: You are not particularly sure on that?
A: *No.*

(I have included questions numbered 54 to 59 in order to show the uncertainty and the forgetfulness of the witness.)

Q66: Did you suggest to him that he hadn't a special Exemption Order for the Sunday night?
A: *I cannot recollect that now.*

Q67: Well, Mr. Shortt will say that, in fact, you did.
A: *I cannot remember whether he had one or not, whether he applied for one or not, I just cannot...*

Q68: Wasn't the complaint in relation to the conduct of Sergeant McPhillips of Muff?
A: *No, my lord, it was related – the complaint – by reason of the fact that he wasn't long in business when the Gardaí inspected his premises and that he felt that if people had stayed over there a lot of the time, that the Gardaí and particularly myself should look most favourably on Mr. Shortt.*

(At this stage the defects in the superintendent's memory were apparent. His answers here, which might strike the reader as being incomplete and disjointed, are the authentic responses he made to the questions. In particular, his response to Q68 is incoherent.)

Q69: Now, you had further correspondence with Mr. Shortt between the 21st April and the 9th June?
A: *That's correct, my lord.*

Q70: And on the 9th June you called out to Mr. Shortt's premises and there you met himself and his wife?
A: *That is correct, my lord, that was at his own premises in Quigley's Point.*

Q71: Had there been anything of significance the evening before that you were aware of in Moville?
A: *Such as...*

Q72: Had there been a drugs seminar in Moville that previous evening?
A: *I was not aware of it.*

Q73: You were not aware of it?
A: *No.*

Q74: Was it not brought to your attention by Mr. Shortt in the course of your meeting on the 9th June?
A: *I have no recollection.*

Q75: You have no recollection?
A: *No.*

Q76 Now, when you called to the premises on the 9th June you say that there was a discussion in relation to drugs, isn't that right?
A: *No, my lord, I didn't say that, but I said that he was running a rave disco dance which I was of the opinion was drug-related.*

Q77: And you say that Mr. Shortt didn't agree with that, but notwithstanding that he had suggested to you that there was not necessarily any relationship between what you describe as a rave dance and drug taking, he did ask you what measures he could take to prevent it ?
A: *He did, my lord, yes, and I then gave him my answer, which I have already stated.*

Q78: And you say that your answer was to suggest to him that the obvious way - the note I made was that the obvious way to prevent any such alleged drugs at a dance would be to cease running that type of dance?
A: *That's correct, my lord.*

Q79: And that he replied, "No way". Well, I must suggest to you, and it will be Mr. Shortt's evidence to this Court should the need arise, that you never suggested that he immediately stop running this type of dance?
A: *My lord, I was very concerned of any drug dealing which would take place in any Garda district in which I would be in charge. I would be duty-bound to investigate any such information in my possession, or if I held the view that drugs may be passing from one person to another in my Garda district. For Counsel to suggest that after I pointed out to Mr. Shortt that I was of the opinion that rave discos were drug-related, I categorically stated and have a clear recollection of having stated to Mr. Shortt that the best way to alleviate any fears of drugs on or about his premises was to stop the type of dance which, in my view, attracted people to do drug dabbling.*

(In the light of Superintendent Kenny's stated abhorrence of the illegal drugs trade and its association with certain types of music and discos I suppose it's fair to assume that, since his transfer to County Meath in August 1992, he has closed down all types of entertainment from which there may be a whiff of illegal drugs trafficking in his district. If he had been District Officer in charge of Rosslare Ferry Port would he also have closed down the port in order to prevent the "passing" of drugs from other countries into Ireland? Would he also have closed down Dublin and Shannon Airports as vast quantities of illegal drugs have also been carried on board aircraft entering these airports?)

Q80: Well now, that is all very interesting, Superintendent, but if you were such a concerned member of An Garda Siochana, how come you were not aware that there had been a drugs seminar in Moville the night before which I understand is within your Garda district or patch?
A: *My lord, if I had been notified or invited to a drugs seminar I would have attended. I was not aware, and I was not invited, and, indeed, I have attended other such meetings in other Garda districts.*

Q81: You say you weren't aware of the meeting in Moville on the night of the 8th June, 1992.
A: *That's correct, my lord.*

Q82: And you say such was your liaison or lack of liaison with people who might run that seminar that you were not aware of it or didn't appreciate that it was in fact being held.
A: *My lord, I was not aware of it. As I said to you, if I had been invited or made aware I would have made myself available.*

Q83: Well, tell me, were any members of An Garda Siochana present at that particular seminar?
A: *My lord...*

Q84: Did you subsequently hear of any Gardaí being present at it, because my instructions are that the seminar was in fact given by members of An Garda Siochana?
A: *My lord, I am not aware.*

Q85: You are not aware?
A: *It wasn't brought to my attention.*

Q1A: To get the matter out of the way you say you were not aware of the seminar in Moville on the previous day, the 8th June 1992?
A: *That is correct, my lord.*

Q2A: My instructions are that that seminar had been given by a number of members of the Garda Siochana, three, possibly, four, and those that were there, Sergeant Jim Moore was one of them. I think he is in court at the moment or certainly was in court before lunch, and also a Sergeant P.J. Hallinan, is that right?
A: *There is a Sergeant Hallinan, alright, yes.*

Q3A: I am told that they were two of the three or four members of the Garda Siochana who had given this particular seminar, does that help you to recall matters in any way or jog your mind in any way?
A: *My lord, I still was not aware of that particular night. Sergeant Moore did work in my district and a Garda, who was then Garda Halloran, was the JLO officer. Now, if they were giving it I was not aware of it. It could have been just on their own or their own idea for that matter, I am not aware.*

(The witness did not seem to be aware of what was going on in his own Garda district. This may have been excusable as one of his Garda told me that Superintendent Kenny was away on holidays during that period and would not return until the 8th June 1992. So one could not expect the superintendent to be aware of goings on among his Gardaí while he was miles away on vacation. However, even that excuse crumbled many months later prior to my appeal when Superintendent Kenny filed an affidavit with the Court of Criminal Appeal stating that he had (conveniently) returned from holidays on the 4th June 1992 just in time to telephone me on Friday morning the 5th June to set up the important meeting several days later on the 9th June. Both I and my wife are absolutely certain that Superintendent Kenny did not, as he alleged in his affidavit, telephone me on the 5th June 1992. It is not every day of the week that members of the public receive phone calls from superintendents so anybody who would receive such a call is highly unlikely to forget.)

Q4A: And you don't believe that this seminar was mentioned or do you in the course of the meeting that took place on the 9th June, 1992?
A: *I have no recollection of it being mentioned. If I had I would have discussed it or sought some information on it with my colleagues.*

Q5A: Because Mr. Shortt will say that when he attended that particular meeting that he effectively had with him an agenda to discuss with you?
(My agenda is outlined in the book. Item 5 on that agenda refers to the drugs seminar on 8th June, 1992.)
A: *That is not so, that was not the reason for our meeting that particular day.*

Q6A: The purpose of the meeting had arisen I think as a result of a complaint that Mr. Shortt was making in relation to the conduct of Sergeant McPhillips?
A: *Not particularly Sergeant McPhillips. As I already outlined to the court he was complaining over his premises being inspected under the Liquor Licensing Laws.*

Q7A: Had you not received a letter of the 8th June sent to you by Fax?
A: *No, my lord, I have no recollection of that.*

Q8A: Was there not a letter of the 8th June sent to you by Fax?
A: *No, my lord, I am not aware of any letter.*

Q9A: You are not aware of any letter. Mr. Shortt will say that he had in fact communicated with you by Fax on the 8th June, 1992?
A: *If that was so, my lord, I certainly would have discussed the Fax with Mr. Shortt on the 9th June, the next day.*

Q10A: Well, I must suggest to you that it in fact was discussed, that there was a number of matters discussed at that meeting on the 9th June and that the main part of the conversation and that the bulk of the conversation and meeting was taken up with the allegations that were being made by Mr. Shortt as regards the behaviour of Sergeant John McPhillips?
A: *The main reason for the meeting was* as a *result of the gardai carrying out inspections on his licensed premises under*

the Liquor Licensing Laws. He did suggest that himself and Sergeant McPhillips at times did not see eye to eye.

Q11A: I think what was being stated by Mr. Shortt was far more succinct than that they did not see eye to eye. I think it was being made abundantly clear to you that as far as Mr. Shortt was concerned he considered the Sergeant's attitude and general approach to be one that was of great upset to him and that he found him a man who was arrogant and dictatorial?
A: *Sergeant McPhillips would have inspected his licensed premises during the course of an inspection carried out by him. On other occasions there were other Gardaí as far as I can recall.*

(His response to this question is again meaningless and incoherent just as in his answer to Q68 earlier.)

Q12A: And you say that you have no recollection of having received a letter of the 8th June, 1992, by Fax?
A: *I have no recollection. I feel if I had of received such a letter I certainly would have had it with me on the 9th June and discussed it with Mr. Shortt.*

Q13A: And you don't accept that the main bulk of the meeting of the 9th June dealt with the attitude or behaviour or demeanour of Sergeant McPhillips?
A: *That is not so my lord. It was, as I have already pointed out to this Court, by reason of the fact that the Gardaí had inspected his licensed premises under the Liquor Licencing Law.*

Q14A: And it is just purely coincidental you say that you called to the premises on the 9th June and it had nothing to do with the Fax that might have been received by you on the 8th June?
A: *That is correct, my lord. I did call on two previous occasions prior to the 9th June, but Mr. Shortt was not there*

and his premises were not open. The reason I called on the 9th June is that I had forewarned Mr. Shortt that I would come to him and discuss the complaints he had made in relation to his premises being inspected.

(Why did the superintendent remain silent about his phone call to me only a few days earlier on the 5th June as alleged in his subsequent Affidavit? Surely that would have clarified things to the court. But then there was no phone call to me on the 5th June 1992, was there?)

Q15A: Tell me, at this meeting of the 9th June, was there any discussion between yourself and Mr. Shortt as regards whether or not the visits by Sergeant McPhillips might have been ordered from a higher level or have the approval of officers at a higher level than Sergeant rank?
A: *I have no recollection. Sergeant McPhillips and indeed any member of the Garda Siochana is quite entitled to inspect any premises at any time if they see so fit.*

Q16A: Because you see Mr. Shortt will say that at the meeting of the 9th June you confirmed that Sergeant McPhillips did not have your approval for his conduct?
A: *That is not so, my lord.*

Q17A: Had there not been a raid on the premises on the night/morning of the 7th cum 8th June?
A: *I am not sure, my lord.*

Q18A: You are not sure?
A: *No, my lord.*

Q19A: Because, you see, again I must suggest to you that that was a matter that was discussed at this particular meeting on the 9th June?
A: *Well, I have no recollection of one, my lord.*

Q20A: And that was a search conducted by Sergeant McPhillips with I think perhaps seven other members of An Garda Siochana?
A: *I would have made the appointment prior to the 9th June I would think a few days in advance to give him - number one, to ensure he was there and number two, that he was aware of my coming, that would be well prior to the 9th June.*

(Perhaps the reader is confused, thinking that I have the above answer out of sequence. Not so, that was the answer which the witness gave to Q20a. Can I now refer you back to his answer to Q14a when counsel for the Defence asked him if it was "purely coincidental that he called to our premises on the 9th June" and his response was "That is correct, my lord." So Superintendent Kenny has given two totally different and contradictory responses to a similar question. Which answer is the truth? One of his answers under oath must be a lie intended to deceive the jury. A lie under oath constitutes perjury which is a very serious criminal offence. However, it seems to me and to a large segment of the public at large that Gardaí and politicians are exempt from prosecution for perjury.

Now we have the witness blurting out an answer to a question he wasn't asked. It seems to me that his mind was running ahead of the questions and he may have felt that he was being trapped. First, the witness tells the Court that the meeting of 9th June was purely coincidental and then he changes his mind and tells the Court that he had set up the meeting a few days in advance. Both are untrue. That meeting was set up by me as a direct consequence of a faxed letter which I transmitted to Superintendent Kenny following the illegal raid the previous day by Sergeant McPhillips and seven other Gardaí searching for illegal drugs in my nightclub. The full text and surrounding details of this fax and the meeting which followed the next day, 9th June 1992 are already outlined.

Firstly, there is absolutely no doubt that I faxed that letter on the 8th June 1992 to Superintendent Kenny at the Garda Station in Buncrana. Subsequent discovery of the fax in the Garda file proves that beyond any doubt. Secondly, I followed up my fax with a phone call an hour later and spoke to Superintendent Kenny. He confirmed to me that he had received the fax and it was then that the day and time for our meeting was fixed. Being a professional accountant I have always been meticulous in keeping notes and records of important events and meetings.

Superintendent Kenny's evidence to the Court stating that he had not received my fax but instead going on to say that it was he, and not I, who had set up the meeting of 9th June 1992, is simply not true. Why would I state in my fax "It is imperative that I meet you as soon as possible" if, according to the evidence given to the court by the superintendent he had spoken to me just a few days earlier and both of us had arranged to meet the day after I sent the fax? It is nonsensical that I would make such a suggestion.

Many of his responses given to the Court prior to this and his many failures to recall events must cast grave doubt on the overall credibility of evidence sworn by Superintendent Brian Kenny. It seemed as though he was making up answers as he went along.)

Q50A: Superintendent, did you ever prepare a list of potential drug dealers?
A: *No, my lord.*

Q51A: And you never furnished such a list to Mr. Shortt if you did not prepare one, clearly?
A: *No, my lord.*

Q52A: Did you ever suggest to Mr. Shortt what he should be looking for?
A: *As I have already stated I had no confidence in Mr. Shortt.*

(Superintendent Kenny had no right to be judgemental and the jury ought to have been instructed to ignore his unhelpful comment. That deliberate comment demonized me and portrayed me in a poor light and obviously diminished my stature and reputation in the eyes of the jury.)

Q53A: Leaving aside whether or not you had confidence in Mr. Shortt or not, did you tell him or did you not tell him what he should be looking out for, isn't the answer no?
A: *That is correct my lord.*

Q54A: Did you discuss with Mr. Shortt any preventative steps that he could take?
A: *At the latter part of the meeting that we discussed the rave disco I had made up my mind then that I was not going to enlist the help of Mr. Shortt in relation to drug dealing, alleged drug dealing, in Quigley's Point and in his own particular premises. I had my reasons for coming to that conclusion.*

Q55A: Well, you say you came to that conclusion and we don't need you to be making these snide suggestions or innuendos for this jury. We will just stick to the facts, please. You didn't?
A: *You asked me why I didn't and I gave you my answer.*

Q56A: Did you discuss the question of putting undercover Gardaí into the premises?
A: *Mr. Shortt had suggested that to me and I declined to discuss that.*

Q57A: Well you are telling me and you are telling his lordship and the jury that Mr. Shortt raised the issue with you of undercover personnel being placed on the premises?
A: *He asked me what would be the normal procedure and I had to say to him in the past we would have put undercover Gardaí to detect any such offences.*

Q58A: And I must suggest to you that not only did Mr. Shortt suggest to you that undercover agents or plain clothes Gardaí should be put into the premises but that you in fact agreed to such a course?
A: *My lord, I have already stated the reasons why I did not take that matter a step further. If I did agree to go that particular way as suggested by counsel, certainly myself or Inspector Lennon on my behalf would have talked to Mr. Shortt on that particular matter.*

(Superintendent Kenny certainly did discuss with my wife and I the introduction of undercover Gardaí into our nightclub. We both agreed with his recommendation and that agreement goes to the very crux of this case.)

Q59A: You see, I must suggest to you that you did say that that is what you were going to do when it was suggested by Mr. Shortt.
A: *No, my lord, I made no such firm decision.*

Q60A: And I must say to you further that Mr. Shortt and his wife assured you that you would have their full support and cooperation?
A: *As I have already stated, my lord, I made no firm decision then.*

Q61A: You made no firm decision then on the 9th June 1992?
A: *That is right, my lord, yes.*

Q62A: Well, when in fact did undercover agents go into the premises first after the 9th June 1992?
A: *It would have been subsequent to the 10th June or the 14th June.*

Q63A: I think perhaps it is the 21st June, is it not?
A: *Inspector Lennon was carrying out that investigation for me and he would have been acting with my approval.*

(That ended Superintendent Kenny's evidence)

Appendix Three
FRANK SHORTT'S EVIDENCE

Examination of Frank Shortt by his counsel Mr. Barry White, S.C.

Q23: You had this meeting with him (Superintendent Kenny) on the 9th June?
A: *That is correct, my lord.*

Q24: I think on the day prior to the 9th June, the 8th of June, there had been a drugs seminar?
A: *That is correct, my lord.*

Q25: And where was that drugs seminar conducted?
A: *The drugs seminar was conducted in a hotel establishment in Moville. The seminar was given by at least three Gardai, there may have been a fourth. It was attended by somewhere in the region of fifty to sixty members of the public and that included my wife and myself.*

Q26: Can you tell his lordship and the jury why yourself and your wife attended that particular seminar?
A: *For two reasons. One was we were aware, like many members of the public, that Ireland was being subjected to a wave of illegal drugs, so we were concerned to find out as much as possible, first of all, for the protection of our own family and secondly, for the protection of my business, The Point Inn.*

Q27: When you saw Superintendent Kenny on the 9th June - perhaps I shouldn't lead you on this - what did that particular meeting deal with?
A: *Among the matters discussed was the seminar referred to, and the second major point of discussion involved the possibility of illegal drugs being in or in the vicinity of my premises.*

Q28: Prior to the seminar being discussed and indeed the possibility of drugs being on your premises being discussed, was there any discussion in relation to Sergeant McPhillips?
A: Yes. *I once again discussed the ongoing attitude of Sergeant John McPhillips towards me and my business.*

Q29: Now, when you discussed the seminar that had taken place on the previous day and when you discussed the possibility of there being drugs on your premises, can you relate to his lordship and the jury as best you can what was discussed in relation to The Point Inn itself, and what was discussed as regards preventative measures that might be taken?
A: *Superintendent Brian Kenny drew the attention of my wife and I to the fact that he had information to the effect that some people were behaving in a suspicious manner in the environment of The Point Inn. In response to that, I suggested to Superintendent Kenny that I would erect a number of posters on the walls inside the nightclub. Those posters would draw the attention of the patrons to the nightclub to the effect that anybody dealing in any fashion whatsoever with illegal drugs, would be dealt with very sternly by the management and would be handed over to the Garda Siochana.*

Q30: And what was the response of Superintendent Kenny towards that suggestion by you?
A: *Superintendent Kenny responded by stating that he didn't think that was a good idea, as it was merely drawing attention to illegal drugs. The question of undercover agents, Garda agents was then discussed and it was clearly agreed that undercover agents would be introduced by the Superintendent at the earliest possible opportunity. I informed the Superintendent there immediately at the meeting that I welcomed such a decision and that I and my staff would co-operate fully with both himself and the undercover Gardaí.*

Q31: Was this meeting a harmonious meeting or was there any acrimony in the course of it at all?
A: *There was no acrimony whatsoever; it was a very harmonious, amicable and friendly meeting and I felt honestly that Superintendent Kenny was convinced of my sincerity and I certainly was convinced of his sincerity.*

Q32: The Superintendent in his evidence has deposed to the fact that he says that he told you the only way to deal with any potential drugs on your premises was to cease the type of discotheque that you were holding and that your response was of a reply of "No way." Have you any comment to make in relation to that, Mr. Shortt?
A: *Superintendent Kenny did not ask me to close my business or premises.*

(The questioning then proceeds along the lines of the inspection of our premises on the night of 22nd June by Inspector Kevin Lennon and the first appearance of the undercover Gardaí in our nightclub on that night.)

Q59: And were you aware of their presence (undercover Gardaí) on the premises on that particular night?
A: *I had instructed, following the meeting of the 9th June which I had with Superintendent Kenny, I instructed all my security staff that undercover Gardaí were going to carry out surveillance on our nightclub, and I advised them all to please give the Gardaí clearance to carry out their work efficiently. In the weekends that followed the meeting of the 9th June, 1992, my security staff on several occasions drew my attention to certain people behaving strangely, and they suggested to me that they resembled undercover Gardaí, so I advised them not to interfere. I told them that I expected the Gardaí would carry out arrests.*

Q60: In particular it has been suggested that yourself and one of your security staff had a discussion apparently in relation

to Garda Mary Finnegan on the particular night of the 6th July, that either you were pointing to her or both of you were pointing to her, and that she was shadowed so to speak around the premises that particular night. Have you any comment to make in relation to that?
A: *Yes, my lord. As I have said in my previous evidence, my security staff had drawn my attention on several occasions to people acting in a strange or unusual fashion. We came to the conclusion that they were, as I stated, undercover Gardaí. However, when they drew my attention to Garda Finnegan as I now know her to be, my security staff stated that she was working alone, that the other undercover agents as we suspected they were undercover Gardaí, that they appeared to be operating in pairs, so we were not quite sure whether this lone woman was a Garda or what she was. So, that is the reason why our security kept surveillance on her.*

Q65: As regards the 27th July, we are aware that again these two members of the Garda Siochana were on your premises. Were you aware of their presence?
A: *Yes, I was aware of their presence and again our security staff were following my instructions to give them a wide berth; we were still expecting arrests to be carried out.*

Q66: And again on the 3rd August, I think we are aware that Garda McMahon and Garda Fowley were on the premises. Were you aware of their presence that night?
A: *Yes, my lord, I was.*

Q67: I think, on that night we are also aware on the evidence that they weren't the only Gardaí that came into the premises prior to the large party of riot police, so to speak?
A: *That is correct, my lord.*

Q68: I think we are told that it was Garda Kelly and Mannion were also on the premises.
A: *Yes, there were two pairs of undercover Gardaí.*

Q69: On these particular nights that we are dealing with, did you observe any of your clientele being arrested by any member of An Garda Siochana?
A: *None at all.*

(My evidence then goes on to describe the environment inside my nightclub in terms of highly technical disco lights, psychedelic beams and machines to pump out artificial fog so as to enhance the overall effect and the dungeon atmosphere.)

Q92: It was suggested by Garda McMahon and indeed by Garda Fowley that on one occasion when they were there, the customers were openly dancing on tables and chairs, and that apparently this was going unchecked by management. Have you any comment in relation to that?
A: *Yes, I do, my lord. There is absolutely no way that I would tolerate 17 or 18 people dancing on any table, let alone remove glasses from between their feet as suggested by Detective Garda McMahon. I would like to state, however, that occasionally the odd person, mainly male, would get up on a table, but would be quickly removed by either myself or security personnel.*

Frank Shortt cross-examined by Mr. Mills, SC for the prosecution

Q93: I think what you were telling his lordship and the jury here, Mr. Shortt, is that you were as concerned as the Gardaí and as parents, let them be from Donegal or Northern Ireland, about how you would identify the use of drugs, how to control it and how to wipe it out.
A: *Yes, that is correct, my lord.*

Q94: Now this drugs seminar that was organised, you say that was organised by the Gardaí or was it just attended by some Gardaí?
A: *At the time I understood it was organised by the Gardaí.*

Q95: What led you to understand it was being run, or shall we say you believed, what made you believe it was being run by the Gardaí?
A: *Because the only lecturers or instructors who I took to number three or four were all members of the Garda Siochana.*

Q96: Did you discover that since then it perhaps wasn't organised by the guards?
A: *I didn't discover that until I heard the evidence the other day by Sergeant Jim Moore.*

(Presumably counsel for the DPP was anxious to emphasise the fact that the Gardaí had not arranged the drugs seminar so as to provide a flimsy alibi for Superintendent Kenny's lack of awareness of the seminar.)

Q97: Anyway, take it as it is, you and your wife attended this conference, is that right?
A: *Yes, that is true, my lord.*

Q98: A one-day conference?
A: *A one-night conference lasting approximately one and a half hours.*

Q99: And were there any other proprietors of discos attending that you knew?
A: *I didn't observe any other proprietors or managers of nightclubs.*

Q100: How many attended, roughly speaking?
A: *My guess was 50 to 60.*

Q101: How many guards do you think were there?
A: *Apart from the three or four instructors, I didn't observe any Gardaí.*

Q102: I take it the purpose of a seminar of this nature is to address disco owners like yourself, parents like some of the people who were there, this was a fairly preliminary and basic kind of information was being given out?
A: *Yes, it was.*

Q103: Can you recall what advice was given out by the lecturers?
A: *During the course of the seminar, the Gardaí passed out these small plastic bags containing samples primarily of cannabis, cannabis in its herbal form and cannabis in resin form, and the purpose in handing them out through the crowd was so that the participants could look at these samples and try to learn to identify what the drug looked like.*

Q104: Any other samples used?
A: *I don't recall any other samples. There certainly weren't any samples of Ecstasy or Lysergide or any of those things. As far as I recall it was solely cannabis.*

Q105: Well, did the lecturer touch upon LSD which is Lysergide and Ecstasy?
A: *As a matter of fact, I very clearly recall a question coming from the floor to one of the instructors to the effect, what about this new drug Ecstasy, to which the response from the instructor was, this is a relatively new form of illegal drug coming on the market, we know very little about it and we don't have any samples.*

Q106: That was said about Ecstasy?
A: *That was the Garda comment about Ecstasy, specifically.*

Q107: In 1992?
A: *That was the 8th of June 1992.*

Q108: And there was no reference to the ease with which identity could be established whether Ecstasy was being used?
A: *I am sorry, I have missed your point.*

Q109: There was no reference to how, by paying attention, how easy it might be to discover whether or not Ecstasy as a tablet was being used?
A: *There were no instructions whatsoever given by the Gardaí as to anything got to do with Ecstasy. There comment was, it is a new drug, it is just recently on the market, we do not have any samples.*

Q110: Well, did they say how it affected the user?
A: *They made no comment whatsoever other than what I have just stated.*

Q114: No reference to the fact that its use by the user is associated with drinking copious amounts of water?
A: *My lord, there was no comment whatsoever in that regard.*

(The next forty six questions dealt with our clientele; where they came from; how they were transported to our nightclub in the open countryside; and so on. This narrative will now pick up the cross-examination that is of relevance to the reader.)

Q161: You have told his lordship and the jury that your belief was that after the meeting with Superintendent Kenny on the 9th June that the guards were going to put into operation undercover agents?
A: *That was my belief, yes, as per the arrangement and agreement with Superintendent Kenny.*

Q162: Well now, I think you said to Mr. White that that was expressly agreed that that would be done. Is it now only a belief?
A: *It was expressly agreed with Superintendent Kenny.*

Q163: It was now expressly agreed that the guards were to take over the undercover operation to your knowledge which you would then communicate to your wife, your children and to all people who work for you in the disco?
A: *That is correct, my lord.*

Q164: And that the Gardaí were to be solely responsible to see what was going on, to make the arrests and it was nothing to do with you whatsoever?
A: *That is correct, my lord. I felt that to interfere in any way might be interpreted by the Gardaí with interference with the guards' instructions.*

Q165: I don't recall Superintendent Kenny having that suggested to him by your counsel, that after that meeting on the 9th of June, you were to stay out of it, the guards would take over any undercover activity and would pick out the drug dealers, arrest them and clean the place up?
A: *Having agreed with Superintendent Kenny at the meeting of the 9th of June 1992, that undercover Garda personnel would enter my establishment, at the meeting I asked the Superintendent would he inform me in advance on the nights the undercover were going in, as it was my intention to co-operate as much as possible with his staff. He did not proffer any advice to me as to how I or my staff were to conduct ourselves.*

Q170: And you contend that you never saw a single transaction of the nature deposed to by the Garda witnesses?
A: *I saw suspicious behaviour but it was not to be interrupted by me or my security staff because we knew the garda undercovers was present and we were expecting arrests to be carried out.*

Q171: So, the whole thing is, to use a modern expression, the arrangement you came to with Superintendent Kenny was a 'cock-up' from the word go, he didn't let you know when they were sending the men in, and that what was going on there, the transactions that were going on there you believed was the gards carrying out their business of dealing with drugs in your premises, is that right?
A: *My lord, as far as I am concerned, it was not, to use the term of counsel a 'cock-up'. I conducted myself and I understand my security staff conducted themselves in accordance with a pre-determined plan namely, to give the undercover Gardaí a clear, shall we call it, shot at any illegal activity going on in our establishment. The fact that the Gardaí did not make an arrest is their affair, it is not mine.*

(The hearing then switched to the visit of Inspector Lennon to our nightclub twelve days after my meeting with Superintendent Kenny on the 9th June. I told the Court that I had informed the inspector of the arrangement which I had entered into with Superintendent Kenny regarding undercovers. Mr. Mills, SC for the prosecution accused me for the first time of lying "there was not a word of truth in it". My immediate response to the Court was: *"My lord, we have heard evidence here today of what transpired between myself and Superintendent Kenny. We also heard evidence last week by Superintendent Kenny that on the day following our meeting, that is the 10th of June, 1992, he instructed Inspector Kevin Lennon to mount a surveillance operation on The Point Inn. When Inspector Lennon visited the premises on the morning of the 22nd June 1992, and requested a private meeting with me, it strikes me as being reasonable that we would have discussed the matter of the undercover operation presently underway in our business that very night."*)

Q187: It would strike the jury *too* that you would be able to tell him that his superior officer, namely the Superintendent had said that undercover agents would be put in place to do the detection, to make the arrests and consequently to clean up, in the belief that drugs were being sold and used in your disco?
A: *It seems obvious to me, your lordship.*

Q188: Are you making a speech now or are you answering a question?
A: *I am endeavouring to answer your question.*

Q189: There was no such reference at that meeting with Inspector Lennon upstairs in your room where your wife and you met him about the Garda plan to come in under cover?
A: *Yes there was.*

Q201: So, according to you, Mr. Shortt, not only did the Superintendent know but the Inspector knew from you on the 22nd June that you knew the guards were going to come in under cover, you expected them and they were there to do the business, of seeing the transactions, making the arrests and putting an end to the corrupt practice, the unlawful activity on your premises?
A: *Yes, my lord. I would like to reiterate that Superintendent Kenny in his evidence told this Court that on the 10th June he instructed Inspector Kevin Lennon to mount a surveillance operation. On the visit of Inspector Lennon of the 22nd June, I confirmed that arrangement with the Inspector.*

Q202: Look, you weren't present when he gave his instructions to the Inspector?
A: *No, I was not, my lord.*

Q203: Well then, how would you have known until the Superintendent gave the evidence that he instructed Lennon to take it up and go for finding out what was going on in your disco – how could you have known that?
A: *Well, it would seem obvious to me that having thirteen days earlier held a meeting with the Superintendent, followed up by a visit from the Inspector, a visit which heretofore I had never received that there obviously had to be an understanding between the Superintendent and his subordinate officer.*

Q204: So what. You say they shouldn't talk to each other about a common object?
A: *On the contrary, my lord, it is quite obvious that they collaborated together.*

Q205: The position is, Mr. Shortt, the Superintendent saw you by calling, not by appointment, he called to your office, isn't that right, or called to see where you were?

(So now we have the prosecutor drop the idea that Superintendent Kenny had made an appointment, yet Kenny was so determined in insisting during his evidence that he had made an appointment to see me on the 9th June 1992.)

A: *The Superintendent received a Fax letter from me on the 8th of June transmitted by fax machine at eleven minutes past twelve midday.*

Q206: Would you go on? Had you set up an appointment for the day he called?
A: *That letter requested the Superintendent to come and meet me and personally inspect my nightclub. The Superintendent ought to have got that Fax on the very same day, the 8th of June, and he met my wife and I at our premises on the day of the 9th of June, 1992.*

(At this point the court rose for lunch. In the afternoon counsel for the prosecution embarked on a determined effort to break down my defence particularly in regard to the agreement on undercover Gardaí which Superintendent Kenny had entered into with my wife and I on Tuesday, the 9th June 1992.)

Q41: Are you seriously expecting his lordship and the jury to accept there was a clear agreement by the senior Garda authorities, starting with the Superintendent and then coming down to the Operations Manager, Detective Inspector Lennon, that the guards would provide undercover surveillance on the premises and in their own way, without reference to you, tidy up what they felt needed to be tidied.
A: *My lord, I have no doubt whatsoever in* my *mind that I had an understanding and an agreement with Superintendent Brian Kenny as of the 9th of June 1992 and my opinion at the time of that meeting was that Superintendent Kenny was acting in the best of good faith and in the interests of my business.*

Q42: That's not quite my question. I accept he was acting in good faith. I think you have been at pains to show that the guards were not acting in good faith but out to single you out for persecution to the exclusion of every other person running a disco. But my point to you is this, are you expecting the jury to believe that you left the Superintendent you believing that you had an express agreement with him that undercover guards would be sent on the premises when the discos were taking place so that they could observe, make the arrests where they deemed it proper and in that way put an end to what they believed was happening on your premises?
A: *My lord, I have no doubt but myself and Superintendent Kenny had a clear understanding in regard to the undercover Gardaí.*

Q43: Well, how could he have an understanding unless it was an agreement?
A: *It was a verbal agreement.*

Q45: Yes, stated to be an agreement?
A: *It was a verbal agreement, a verbal understanding.*

Q46: I accept that, but expressly providing for what the guards would do and what duties you would perform so that they could so do it?
A: *I was given no instructions by Superintendent Kenny as to what my function in the particular surveillance operation was to be. Nor was I told by Superintendent Kenny as to precisely what the undercovers would do.*

Q51: Did you expect them to share with you the Garda strategy, whatever it might happen to be, to make an arrest or number of arrests?
A: *Frankly, my lord, I thought I might have received some form of cooperation. After all, I was cooperating. I had hoped that I might get some cooperation from them.*

(The prosecution continued to badger me for a further hour about the undercover agreement. My responses were unhesitatingly clear: "*I have expressed before this court on several occasions that there was a clear arrangement between myself and Superintendent Kenny established at our meeting on the 9th June, 1992, and I left it to the Superintendent to carry out his police work without any interference from me. I felt that for us to interfere in any way would or could be construed as interfering with the course of justice.*" This, more or less, concluded my cross-examination by prosecuting counsel.)

Appendix Four
LETTERS TO NORA OWEN

Sally ~~Natasha~~ Shortt,
The Old Rectory,
Clar,
Redcastle,
Co. Donegal.
Tel: 077-82400.
20.8.96.

Dear Mrs. Owens,
    I am more than concerned about my husband Frank's present situation in Mountjoy.
A man of 61½ yrs locked up 19½ hours a day in a prison where the average age is 20 yrs. I feel he is too old and unfit for such a rigorous routine. He does suffer from back + other medical problems. As a nurse I know that lack of exercise, lack of space + fresh air, a well balanced diet will lead to chronic ill health. In society we are constantly trying to improve conditions for the elderly, why not in Mountjoy? The present regime there, may not effect the average 20yr old but it is going to have a detrimental effect on my husbands health - long term I know, because I work with the elderly. I am ~~therefore begging~~ you to give some

consideration to Jeannie's present ...when

The knock-on effects over the last eighteen months has had a devastating affect on each and everyone of us. Mentally, socially & financially we are all bankrupt. My family are disintegrating around me, and I don't know how to handle it anymore.

I am now asking you Joe the s... of myself and all my five children, to please do somethin... to help us.

I look forward to a little sunsh...

Yours sincerely,
Sally Shortt.

The Old Rectory,
Clar,
Redcastle,
Co. Donegal.
11·11·96

Dear Mrs. Owen,
As you know my husband Frank is now into the last seven months of his three year prison sentence. During all of this time he has never been allowed home for a week-end with us, nor allowed visit me in hospital following major surgery several months ago. I am writing to advise you that on the 30th of this month, we will be celebrating our 29th wedding anniversary. In this day and age this says much for our relationship and our family. Also, in January Frank will be sixty two years of age.

I feel that Frank and the family have suffered enough. He was not granted the concession of an open prison, notwithstanding the fact that this was promised him on the evening of your visit to the Training Unit, 29th March 1996. Had that promise been honoured Frank would have merited a substantial remission of his sentence.

I sincerely request you to please release Frank, now, on compassionate grounds. At this stage of our lives time runs out rapidly, and our children have already started to leave home, and make their own lives. Frank's release now would be a wonderful gift, not just for both of us on our anniversary, but also for the children, particularly the younger ones who have suffered the distress of an absent father at such a formative stage in their development. Sometimes I wonder if they will ever break through the hurt and anguish that they have experienced over the last couple of years. If not for our sakes then for the sake of our children, I am earnestly asking you to grant Frank his full release.

Yours sincerely,
Sally Shortt.